UNDERSTANDING
NEURO
PLASTICITY
AND NEURO
DIVERSITY
IN THE CLASSROOM

To order our books please go to our website www.criticalpublishing.com or contact our distributor Ingram Publisher Services, telephone 01752 202301 or email IPSUK.orders@ingramcontent.com. Details of bulk order discounts can be found at www.criticalpublishing.com/delivery-information.

Our titles are also available in electronic format: for individual use via our website and for libraries and other institutions from all the major ebook platforms.

CRITICAL
PUBLISHING

UNDERSTANDING
NEURO PLASTICITY
AND **NEURO DIVERSITY**
IN THE CLASSROOM

A Handbook
for SENCos
and Teachers

EDITED BY ANITA DEVI AND SUE JAGGER

First published in 2025 by Critical Publishing Ltd

British Library Cataloguing in Publication Data
A CIP record for this book is available from the British Library

ISBN: 978-1-915713-99-5

This book is also available in the following e-book formats:

EPUB ISBN: 978-1-916925-00-7
Adobe e-book ISBN: 978-1-916925-01-4

Text and cover design by Out of House Limited
Project Management by Newgen Publishing UK

Critical Publishing
3 Connaught Road
St Albans
AL3 5RX

www.criticalpublishing.com

Contents

Dedication

We dedicate this book to:

- the children, young people and families who have shaped our hearts, minds and souls;

- to colleagues and employers (past and present) for nurturing our professional curiosity;

- to you, the reader, for being part of the ongoing journey of growth.

Acknowledgements

From Anita: What truly makes the biggest difference in our lives? Love. Faith inspired me to put forward a proposal for this book and hope fuelled me ... hope in the difference it will make for the people of today and tomorrow. But ultimately, Love carried me (and Sue) to completion. So, I want to acknowledge family and friends (the gone, the living and the yet to come). You all have shared and continue to share your hearts and lives with me. This is such a blessing! This is Love and I am grateful. Most of all, Y'shua, you will always be my first love, my confidante and my strength (HPiTP).

From Sue: Teaching is the most rewarding job there is, and I would like to thank everyone who takes the time to understand their students and to help them along their journey of learning. To all those staff, parents and students who have supported me as a student of teaching throughout my career – thank you. Anita, thank you for having the faith in me that has enabled us to go on an adventure of writing together; it has been a wonderful time of growth. But most of all, my love and gratitude goes to my family, my husband Gary, and our children Ellis and Ellen, who never fail to inspire us. Thank you for enabling me to have the time and space to explore the ideas within this book and to talk endlessly about learning.

From both of us: We are grateful to the team at Critical Publishing. We especially feel indebted to Lily Harrison, Assistant Editor, for her unerring guidance and support as we have written this book.

About the editors

Anita Devi

Anita Devi is a former SENCo, senior leader, school improvement advisor and local authority SEND advisory teacher. She has a wealth of experience in developing leaders of learning, and her own teaching career spans early years to postgraduate education both in the UK and overseas. In 2017, she was awarded the prestigious international Influential Educational Leaders Award for her contribution to the SEND workforce pipeline strategy which supports the development of professionals from initial teacher training to advanced and experienced SENCos. Anita has contributed to several publications, was awarded her PhD thesis on the career trajectory of a SENCo in 2022, and is currently a Changemaker Education Consultant and Founding CEO of #TeamADL and #365send.

Find out more about Anita at www.anitadevi.com

Sue Jagger

Sue Jagger is a former literacy consultant, primary deputy head and secondary assistant head. She is currently Head of English and a literacy co-ordinator at a large secondary school. As a literacy consultant and link tutor for a SCITT, Sue has had the privilege of working alongside teachers to develop and share effective pedagogy. After 26 years in the classroom, Sue still believes in the excitement of learning and thoroughly enjoys teaching.

About the contributors

Amanda Kirby has extensive experience in the field of neurodiversity. She has run a clinical and research centre, is the CEO of Do-IT Solutions and has developed web-based screening tools in education. Amanda is an emeritus professor with more than 25 years' research in the field of neurodiversity. She is a medical doctor and also holds a PhD. Amanda has published over ten books, including *Neurodiversity and Education* and *Neurodiversity at Work*, the latter of which won the Business Book Awards 2022. With more than 100 published research papers, Amanda's work has significantly impacted on understanding of education and employment. She has a personal connection to neurodiversity, being neurodivergent herself and having many neurodivergent close family members, and this has driven her enduring commitment to societal change, including being Chair of the ADHD Foundation.

Sarah Moseley is a literacy and inclusion specialist focusing on empowering all learners, embracing neurodiversity and SEND. She provides face-to-face or online training, consultancy, information and support for professionals and families from all sectors. She is passionate about making a positive difference to the lives, attitudes and outcomes of those neurodiverse learners who may struggle to learn. She has over 25 years' knowledge and experience within special and mainstream education up to headteacher level, as well as a solid research background rooted within the psychology of learning that includes a Master's and PhD in special education.

Mark Stibbe has been teaching and writing about recovering from the trauma caused by ruptured attachment to our parents for over three decades and has written *I Am Your Father*. He has given special focus to boarding school trauma and has also written *Home at Last*. His novels also deal with these issues. *A Book in Time* (winner of the 2020 Page Turner Awards) is about the longing for a lost mother's love. *House of Dreams* is about recovering from boarding school trauma – especially abandonment. His recent book *Fathers* won the General Non-fiction Award at the New York Book Festival. Mark is a full-time writer who lives with his wife Cherith and their two Labradors in Kent.

Foreword

We love the way that we are wired for transformation and for learning from the moment we are born into this marvellous and dangerous space called life. We are incredibly made, and from birth to age two we are told that our brains can form around 700 new connections per second as we make sense of it all. This plasticity in our brains, we are told, spikes again around puberty, but remains to some degree with us all our lives. More than facts and data, we initially learn what we now call emotional intelligence, connections, love and a secure base. These key foundations enable us to build our unique library of knowledge of self, others and the world around us. This process can be full of joy and discovery. The joy of learning has motivated both editors of this book on their mission as enablers of others in the excellent practice of education.

We could stop there, and all is well. But as we know, cold winds blow, and the dangers of life can sometimes throw us an unforeseen curveball. Alongside pleasant experiences, many have known acute trauma, felt abandonment, developed poor attachment to a caregiver and experienced abuse of many kinds. I would like to introduce you now to someone who taught us much of this sad side of life. Meet Ryan; Ryan will not look you in the eye for long, but he is acutely aware and vigilant of whatever is happening. If he smiles his mouth moves but there is no light in his eyes. Instead of loving and secure early years, he had suffered neglect, emotional detachment and exposure to violence. His world was chaotic and unsafe, and he carried that world around with him like a backpack that he could not take off. Any toy he would break, or he would use play figures to fight each other. He has no empathy or thoughts of others as the connections were not formed by any significant attachment. Although mentally capable and articulate, he stumbles in learning as he finds himself unable to regulate his emotions or concentrate on tasks in hand. He presents as defiant and oppositional and so is often disciplined at school or excluded. He is volatile and can be violent, yet is acutely vulnerable and easily led. Every cell in him is crying out to be loved, to be accepted and to belong, yet he does not have the scaffolding or tools to express that, let alone experience it. Deep down, his view of himself is in a prison of shame, built as a high wall of protection yet holding him captive. In his words, '*I am bad*'.

You too may know a Ryan; he may be in your classroom, your community or even your home. Each Ryan may have a different story, but the result is the same: learning is impaired, and all of life is seen through a darkened and distorted lens. The knowledge of self, the sense of identity and purpose, is caught in a toxic loop of self-hatred. To consistently love and therapeutically care for Ryan we think has been the biggest challenge of our lives, with many tears shed on the way. Your journey as an educator or carer may be far more acute than ours, and if so, we applaud you and wish you well with all of our hearts, but we can also be pragmatic as well.

Just sometimes a book is written at an opportune time when what is needed is a calm voice of balance and hope. We see that in this book: a strategy for learning that is as simple as ABC, considering the neuroplasticity of our brains alongside the primary need for healing of our emotional base and identity. We are after all multifaceted and if our inner world of feelings and emotion is not healthy, we are ill-equipped to train our thinking in helpful and constructive ways. Furthermore, this book considers who we are and how we see ourselves as integral to a connected community, learning to walk into freedom for ourselves and those we have the privilege to walk alongside.

This has to be helpful not just for Ryan, but for each of us who are fearfully and wonderfully made.

Dave and Mandy Eyeington
Parents of Katie, Nathanael, Josiah and Thomas
In-laws of Nathan
Grandparents of Elijah and Olivia
Foster carers of Ryan and 28 other children who have enriched
our lives more than they know

Icon index

Each chapter includes the following features.

Structural element within each chapter	Icon	What this means ...
Chapter aims	◎	Around the ABC model, each chapter has key aims and/or questions that will be addressed
Reflection	?	Moments to ponder and consider
Case study	💬	Case studies provide examples
Application	x↑ 6x	Practical approaches and tools to apply
Key takeaways	📝	Key points to consider
Key question	?	To further dialogue with others

Introduction

This is OUR book. It is not just about us as editors or those who wrote and contributed, but also about you – the practitioner in the classroom, living out the day-to-day role of teaching. The value of this book is not just in the researching, writing, editing or even reading. The treasure of this book is in the applying.

Neither of us claims to be an 'expert', but through our professional curiosity we have discovered something.

How this book came together

Like most discoveries, it started with a question: while we accept the notion of neurodiversity in the classroom, surely with the way humans are created and develop, there has to be in-built mechanisms to support neurodiversity? Let us qualify this with an example. Most babies are born with 300 bones. However, as they mature into adults, these fuse together to around 206 bones, which make up approximately 15 per cent of body weight. So, in effect a baby has nearly 100 bones more than an adult! This is the type of conversation on human development plasticity that is missing from our classrooms when looking at neurodiverse needs.

Following the question, we found people who had a heart to help us discover. These were individuals who came from very different walks of life and experience. Based on the different dimensions of the human personality and their specialism, we gave each contributor a specific focus. We never met as a whole group, but what astounded us most when the contributions came in was the common threads between the chapters.

Now it's your turn! As you read the book, seek out common threads between the chapters. We encourage a full read from cover to cover first and then dip in and out as required. Invest time in going back to the reflective questions. Share the case studies, citing the source of course. Who knows, it may encourage others to discover too. Content in each of the chapters could also be used to shape continuous professional development in your setting.

As we've talked to people about this book, we've often been greeted with the response, '*Oh you mean growth mindsets?*' and our resounding reply has always been '*No*'. Growth mindsets are about 'attitude'. Neuroplasticity is about using neural feedback in the brain to create new and different neural pathways. As educators, we have steered away from the medical science of this and look at what this would mean in the classroom.

What we state in the Epilogue holds true – this is just the beginning of discovery. We know there is still SO much to uncover.

We conclude this introduction with **the voice of learners**, which we have structured into a poem. These thoughts were received from students when we asked them about themes from this book and their experience of the classroom.

Do you know?

I know what to expect,

But that doesn't matter.

I don't know if there will be a clicking noise from a pen,

or if the lights are too bright,

the noise too loud or the room too hot.

Sensory overload, so I am told.

Worry I experience.

But I don't have time or space

to think about this ...

Impulsive anxiety, I'm told.

I hear a voice shout ...

my voice loud and deafening.

I hear a door slam

and then realise I am on the other side of it.

Outside once again.

I walk and return ...

same room,

same people,

same lesson,

different moment ...

now I can think clearly.

A different approach

To change my way of thinking

that is what I need.

Thank you for being part of OUR book journey.

Anita and Sue

1 The basics: using an ABC approach

ANITA DEVI

Introduction

As a pupil in school, I was taught to read by learning the alphabet first. I have virtually no recall as to how I transitioned from knowing these ordered 26 segments of grapheme knowledge into fluent reading and writing. But I did. At some point I wired my brain to connect sensory input (recognising the letters) to thoughts (connecting concepts and words) to speech (expressing coherent sentences to others) to a mark on the page (sharing new ideas in printed format). As a teacher in school, I taught others to read using a structured format of 44 phonemes, connecting these to graphemes and eventually fluent printed text. I vividly recall learning to do this and, to be honest, how hard I found it. It was not the way I had learnt to read and write, but it was the way I needed to teach to ensure all learners could grasp the English language and use it widely to fulfil their human potential throughout different stages in their lives. My pupils still needed to eventually learn the 26 letters in order, as it is used for many things such as accessing a word in the dictionary, alphabetical lists in directories or tube stations and writing reference lists for academic essays. The application of using alphabetical lists, for most, has become automated into a habit. This book is about cultivating the habit of change, so it makes sense to use an ABC model.

Chapter aims ◎

This chapter addresses seven questions, around three core themes.

Activate agency

1. Why does choice matter?

2. Is making choices an innate skill or one that requires nurturing and practice?

Breakthrough

3. How flexible are our brains?

4. What does transformation look like in the everyday?

Clarity on personal identity

5. Where does personal identity fit into the curriculum?

6. Labels or life – which has the greater potency?

And finally

7. How can we best connect agency, breakthrough and clarity into a single framework?

Reflection ⑦

Before reading further, take some time to consider these seven questions.

» Which words resonate most for you? Pick three of the seven questions and make notes on your response.

» Are there any questions you would add?

The three themes of agency, breakthrough and clarity are important. You will see them featured throughout the subsequent chapters of this book, so it is important to gain a deeper understanding of each before they are applied to different domains of human development.

Activate agency

I would argue you spend 98 per cent of your life making decisions or solving problems. I have no actual data to prove this, but think about everything you have done today. How many decisions have you made? How many problems have you solved? This extends from the basics of what you might eat or wear each day to the bigger life decisions such as buying a house or applying for a job. Some decisions and problems need to be resolved urgently or are time limited; others give us time to linger and sometimes avoid. The same outward actions can have different levels of decision-making gravity. For example, a confident speaker in a classroom may choose their words wisely, but experience and knowledge will enable them to automate this process to some degree. Imagine now a couple on their first date, both trying to think and decide what to say to the other person. In other contexts, they both may be very articulate, but in the newness of that moment, connectivity between thought and sound production can get lost.

CASE STUDY ☺

Not letting the environment shape ability

There has been a lot of research (Evans et al, 2018; Waters et al, 2014; West et al, 2010; Zeedyk et al, 2003) on how challenging pupils find the transition from primary school to secondary school. In one local authority where I worked as an advisory teacher, we decided to take a different approach. We asked the pupils' future secondary teachers to come and jointly assess with their current primary teachers the level of speaking and listening skills for each pupil. The formal assessment scores and descriptors were shared with the pupils. On the whole, pupils in Year 6 were confident at expressing their opinion, asking questions and explaining ideas. As they moved into secondary school, it was tempting to let the newness of the experience and environment curb their level of speaking. However, because they knew their teachers had seen them excel in speaking previously, and these teachers could encourage and remind pupils of this, we saw less of a dip in oracy skills during the transition compared to previous years. As the pupils were speaking more in class, their learning accelerated. This is an example of where intentional decisions were taken to prevent regression, but also an example of where two active choices came into play: firstly, not allowing the external situation to impact on the internal; and secondly, using external stimuli (the teacher) to strengthen the internal, reminding pupils of their ability to give verbal expression to their ideas. This is significant since over the last two decades we have seen an increasing number of children struggle with speaking and listening, especially post pandemic (2020–22) (Speech and Language UK, 2023). Ask yourself how much space you create in your classroom for speaking and listening. Speech is an external expression of what students are thinking and perceiving internally.

Reflection ⑦

»   Consider the internal and external environments in your classroom. What patterns of co-dependency can you identify?

»   Which one is the stronger influencer and why?

»   Is there anything you would want to change about the relationship between internal and external environments in your classroom?

Deconstructing agency

According to the Oxford Dictionary, agency is intentional 'action or intervention producing a particular effect'. When you make decisions or try to solve problems, more often than not there is a defined desired outcome. Agency involves choice. Many actions and outcomes are simultaneously possible. When teaching this to pupils, I call this a multi-flow map. The multi-flow map serves to show that while you can't always control everything that happens, the choices you make matter.

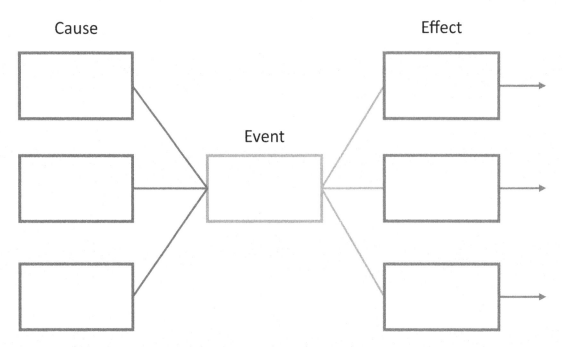

Figure 1.1 *Multi-flow map, highlighting how many causes may lead to a single event, and from this single event, many consequences may follow*

Application

» Think about how you can use this multi-flow map in the classroom to teach a topic or even resolve a dispute from the playground.

Reflection

» Consider the curriculum in your setting. How do you actively teach learners about making choices? Do you break down the big-arc decision into small steps? For example, if you want your pupils to write a story, you might provide them with a scaffold to help them first define the characters and make choices about their personalities. The scaffold structure can also include space for choices around context and different stages of the plot. Another example could be that you need pupils to demonstrate XYZ research skills in history or science. But you allow them to choose the topic of interest so they can demonstrate those skills. This last example brings together differentiation and personalisation.

A good example to illustrate breaking something down into smaller steps and making choices is careers education. A learner expresses a desire to be X when they grow up (replace X with doctor, plumber, engineer, etc). Working backward from being X, the learner has to work out what steps, qualifications, experience and contacts are needed to achieve X.

I believe decision making and problem-solving are learnt skills. This being the case leads me to therefore ask, why are some people better at decision making and problem-solving than others? You might argue this is a loaded question. I agree; however, this means we can change this for all.

Making wise choices, decision making and problem-solving are learnt skills. They are strengthened through the repetition loop, that is, practice and failure, where we understand why something hasn't happened or isn't working and then try something different.

CASE STUDY 💬

In England, the inspectorate team in 2019 gave school leaders the freedom to define the Curriculum Intent for their setting. Obviously, this needed to be within the framework of the 2014 national curriculum. However, what school leaders had was an opportunity to place core skills such as decision making and problem-solving at the heart of learning (Devi cited in Snape, 2024). Both of these are processes, and if applied well they have the potential to connect great teaching (Coe et al, 2014) with learner agency.

Decision making involves a mixture of intuition and rational thinking, along with critical factors such as personal biases and blind spots. Deconstructing decision making reveals eight high-level steps that run in a continual loop:

1. recognising there are options, and a choice needs to be made;

2. knowing what they are;

3. determining a criterion to either eliminate some options or conversely select one/ several;

4. acting on the decision made;

5. adapting with flexibility to unknowns as the decision is acted upon;

6. accepting the consequences of the decision;

7. evaluating the choice/s made, the process and the outcome, as well as learning from it;

8. remembering the experience and learning for next time.

We all make choices, but in the end, our choices make us.

Ken Levine (nd)

Doing nothing is still a decision and choice. Decisions require energy and mental space; hence, over time some decisions become automated, freeing up brain hardware and software to take on more decisions or bigger decisions. However, this can only happen if there is practice, repetition and rehearsal. With rehearsal or practice, would students in today's world of high-paced information feel overwhelmed?

Problem-solving is the ability to find solutions to difficult and often complex situations. Usually the risk factor is higher than just making a decision. Problem-solving embraces decision making as a subset of processes, and it additionally requires:

* accurate knowledge of the problem;

* assessment of the risk, issues or consequences;

* finding a range of options;

* moving into decision-making mode.

There is a linear process to this. If, for example, the problem is perceived slightly differently to what actually exists, this could lead to different options being explored and ultimately different solutions adopted.

Reflection ⑦

Think back to a lesson you taught last week.

» How much choice, decision making and problem-solving did the learners engage in?

» Was it enough or too much?

» What would you do differently in hindsight?

Chalkiadaki (2018) groups the broad range of twenty-first-century skills into four main categories:

1. personal skills;

2. social skills;

3. information and knowledge;

4. digital literacy.

Interestingly, all four categories involve a dimension of decision making and problem-solving, with choice being at the centre.

Choice is critical, and you will see that the titles of the next six chapters all pose an alliterated question of choice.

Breakthrough

CASE STUDY 🔊

Metaphor 1

A farmer seeks to plant a fresh crop, so he needs to plough the land first. As he manoeuvres his tractor through the soil, it becomes stuck. As he keeps pressing down on the accelerator, the tracker tyre embeds itself deeper into the soil. The repetitive spinning sinks the tractor further into the ground on the same track. Eventually, the farmer next door comes along and places a wedge under the tyre. This gives it leverage for the tyre to come out and the tractor releases itself to move on and make new tracks.

Reflection ❓

» How would you relate the tractor story to the rewiring of thought processes?

» Can you name any stuck-tractor learners in your classroom?

» What would act as a wedge to release them from the same patterns of behaviour?

Often, rewiring the brain involves recognising stuck patterns of thought and intentionally changing track, not just driving over and over the same old track.

CASE STUDY 🔊

Metaphor 2

A city worker leaves for work at the same time every day. Wearing the same outfit each day, she stands at the same bus stop every day. En route to work, she picks up a cup of coffee and doughnut from the same café. This city worker clocks out of work at the same time each day. On one occasion, the bus drivers decide to go on strike. The city worker now has to walk. As she does, she notices the parks on the way. She sees a shortcut through a street that has the most beautiful gardens, and she comes across a new bakery that sells the best tea and croissants. This has changed her day!

While routine is helpful, does it stop us from seeing other options and being creative? Does competency in decision making and problem-solving make you better at handling surprises or curveballs?

Reflection ⑦

» How would you relate the city worker story to a learner attending school or college?

» What made the difference to the city worker and how can you relate this to your classroom?

» Should novelty be a daily experience or once in a blue moon, and why?

Habits are powerful, but they can also create situations where individuals are stuck. As a teacher, how do you strike a balance in the classroom between innovative thought and repetitive behaviours, which build discipline and muscle memory, and behaviours that keep learners rooted and stuck? A few years ago, I was leading a training day for youth leaders in our local community. We decided to call the training day 'roots and wings'. We wanted the youth leaders to make the young people feel they belonged (rooted), but equally they needed to stretch each member to fly and spread their wings. Not only did these youth leaders have to continually reflect on this balance, but they also recognised that in an inclusive world, one size does not fit all. Therefore, what might be balance for one young person is not the same for another.

Application 🎲

Think about 'roots and wings' now in the context of your classroom.

» List which aspects continue to support learners to feel safe and rooted.

» Which features enable learners to stretch and go further?

» Is there balance?

Every situation you come across warrants a fresh look at what constitutes the balance.

Breakthrough is about recognising you do not live in a fixed state. Imagine yourself at the centre of a community. You are changing and so are different elements around you.

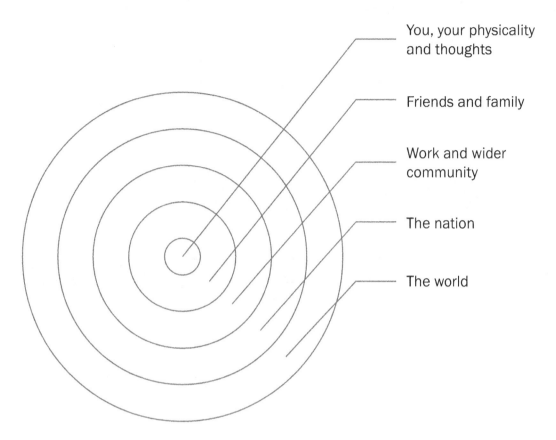

You, your physicality and thoughts

Friends and family

Work and wider community

The nation

The world

Figure 1.2 *Continuous circles of change*

We were created for change and growth. Imagine a newborn baby with all 300 bones. As this baby grows and matures into an adult, the bones blend together to form 206 bones. I often wonder what impact this reduction in bones has on the brain, as it controls thought, memory, emotion, touch, motor skills, vision, breathing, temperature, hunger and every process that regulates our body, while simultaneously working with the spinal cord that extends to make up the central nervous system. But clearly less is more. In terms of the mind, this is known as subtractive psychology. In our minds, we form connections and start grouping concepts so we recall themes rather than individual items. Growth is about both acquisition and loss. Both processes are healthy, but the challenge comes when we are stuck.

Reflection ⑦

»   How many of your learners see growing and stretching as a challenge, as opposed to recognising that being stuck in one place doing the same thing over and over is the greater challenge?

»   How do you contribute to hearts and minds that welcome growth as part of the natural process of change?

Application ▦

» How do you communicate and model change in the classroom?

In my classroom, I would often change one or two things in the environment at the end of the school day, such as move a poster off the wall and place it on another wall or move my desk. The next morning, as the children came in and I was taking the register, the pupils would have to look around the room and guess what had changed. With older children, I would often ask them, '*What is your relationship to change?*' At first, they would look confused with responses such as, '*Miss, change is not a person*'. But over time they learnt to communicate some very insightful responses to themselves and each other.

Breakthrough is a sudden dramatic and important discovery or development: a child's first words, their first step, hopping or catching a ball for the first time. Adult dancers have breakthroughs all the time. For months, they invest time in practising a certain flip, failing to land properly. And then one day, it happens and then again and again until they can't remember a time when they couldn't do it.

A speaker once said to me, '*An amateur does a task until they get it right; a professional or expert does a task knowing they will get it right every time*'. This is the power of excellence, as opposed to perfection. Our bodies, brains and emotions all experience breakthroughs. The question is, do you create space for the breakthrough?

Minor breakthroughs occur in the wider context of child–adult development. Literacy specialists would call this a person's main narrative arc. Your arc began at birth and continues until you die, and different periods along the arc are critical periods for development. For example, most babies around the globe start walking around the age of one, puberty happens in a certain phase of life and so on. These defined development spurts cannot be ignored.

What happens when natural development is undone through a lack of balance?

There is mounting evidence about the different effects of gaming on young people. Various research highlights cognitive, behavioural, social, physical, neurochemical and addictive impacts. While the *Diagnostic and Statistical Manual of Mental Disorders* (DSM-V) does not recognise 'internet gaming disorder', there is growing evidence to show how the human brain becomes rewired to crave instant gratification, and fast-paced and unpredictable activities (Koepp et al, 1998). Sharing his experience in *Brain & Life Magazine* in 2014, Anthony (aged 17), who played games 18 hours a day for two years, said the following: '*I never saw my real friends. I gained weight, became lazy, and spent nearly all of my time slumped over my computer*'. The article also visually highlights how gaming changes the brain. Magnetic resonance imaging (MRI) studies on the brains of 18 college students in China (with a control group) showed that in just two weeks students lost activity in key functions of the brain, including locus of judgement, decision making and impulse control. While these studies focus on negative impacts, what this shows is the brain is not fixed and just as gaming can reduce activity through rewiring, other activities have the potential of rewiring to increase activity. O'Sullivan et al (2019) challenge fixed-state medical models of language disorder, suggesting that alternative therapy approaches that rewire the brain are supporting functional recovery to re-establish brain networks. As an educator, I find this significant for the classroom. Instead of accepting diagnosis as a fixed state, this kind of research plus anecdotal case studies is showing us that breakthrough and rewiring is possible. Understanding the creation model characteristics behind the medical model of diagnosis is taking us closer to a social model of inclusion, where we accept, but also hope for something better. There is much to discover in this field in terms of the how, but the basic premise remains: the brain is not in a fixed state. This means the body is not in a fixed state either and nor is the mind.

Recognising that the brain, body and mind are not in a fixed state implies also that transformation is a part of everyday life. So, in the classroom how do you distinguish between learning and transformation?

Learning implies the acquisition of knowledge or skills, while transformation implies change. The two are interlinked, but this needs to be intentional. For example, it is possible to acquire new knowledge, but this does not change you. Equally, an experience may change you, but you may choose not to learn anything from it.

CASE STUDY ⊛

Having taught in different contexts over the last 40 years, I'm often asked what's my why. My answer has been consistent and clearly articulated for the last 30 years. It is the joy of learning. I always describe this 'joy' as much more than just a 'lightbulb' moment. It's actually a transformative moment, when learning changes something in the individual. The change may be physical (eg when I taught PE or dance), it can be in the mind (eg ways of critical thinking and applying mathematics) or it may be in the heart (eg increased compassion towards others). What we do as educators is far more than impart knowledge; we change lives.

Reflection ⑦

» Write or draw your model of learning. You can find my version in my book for early career teachers (Devi, 2020).

» Where does transformation fit in your model of learning?

» While writing end-of-year reports, do you focus on learning, transformation or both?

Clarity on personal identity

If transformative learning is perceived as desirable, then logic dictates a necessity to ask the fundamental question, who am I?

The body, mind, intelligence, character, personality, morals, culture and emotions are all subject to change and seasons. Therefore, a part of all learners is constantly changing. However, there has to be an aspect that is consistent. At the turn of the century Zohar and Marshall (2000) introduced the term spiritual intelligence (SQ) to determine a conscious level of meaning and purpose, using adaptive principles to maintain stability in a changing world. Others like Draper (2011) focus on choices of SQ (eg finding meaning in the meaninglessness, hope in despair, reconciliation in alienation and wholeness in fragmentation), whereas McGreal (2017), citing Emmons (2000), refers to the transformative process of achieving integrated wholeness. Whatever focus is adopted to consider SQ, the undeniable assertion is that there is a part of the human construct that doesn't change and goes beyond the body, mind and heart functionalities. Some call this Spirit (capital S), others life and some breath. I personally like breath, because it has a binary modality – it is there, or it isn't. A body without breath is simply a corpse; a mind and heart cannot function without breath.

You might be inclined to ask, why does this matter? This creates a basis for our identity.

•   '*I am tall, fair skinned, with x features*' – these are all labels pertaining to the body.

•   '*I am smart, good at art, friendly*' – these are labels pertaining to the mind.

•   '*I am kind, compassionate, friendly*' – these are labels pertaining to the heart.

I breathe means I live and as long as I live, I have life! This framework steers you towards purpose, whereas labels pertaining to the body, mind and heart all relate to a plan. Legacy, longevity and sustainability operate when defining purpose comes before the plan. Obviously, we need both, but plans are better when built around a purpose. Plans can change, even while the purpose remains the same.

How often do you encourage students to seek out their purpose? Or are you constantly pushing the need for a plan on them?

Connectivity

Agency, breakthroughs and clarity (ABC) do not operate in a vacuum. They are interdependent. Agency often leads to breakthrough, which enhances clarity. Equally, clarity can increase agency for breakthrough. As such, I would encourage you to view these three constructs as connected.

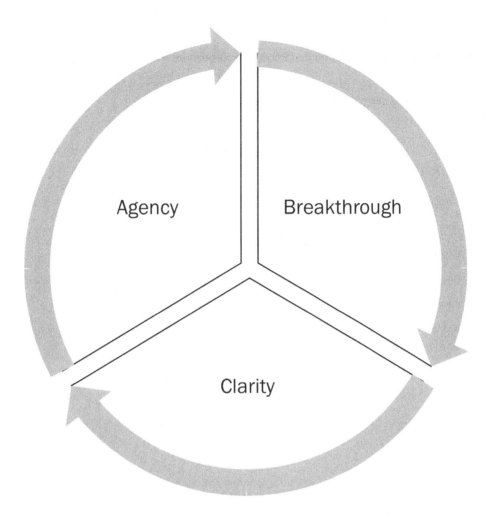

Figure 1.3 *ABC connectivity*

Throughout the subsequent chapters you will see the ABC model applied to the practitioner/ educator or learner. As already stated, the premise of the next six chapters is choice based around different aspects of child/human development.

Summary

In this chapter, I have explored seven questions around the three constructs of agency, breakthrough and clarity (ABC). I have provided case studies and metaphorical examples plus a few activities to extend reflective thought in the classroom. Additionally, I have provided models for thinking (Figure 1.1), observing (Figure 1.2) and connecting (Figure 1.3). Finally, I have established a foundation for other learned contributors to expand upon in subsequent chapters.

Reflection ⑦

» What are your key takeaways from this chapter and how will you apply them to yourself and others?

Key takeaways 📖

It is my hope that you take away the following seven ideas from this chapter.

1. Giving others choice and making decisions is empowering.

2. Choice, decision making and problem-solving are learnt skills.

3. The brain (central controlling system) is not fixed and therefore can be rewired.

4. Learning and transformation work together for maximum impact.

5. Asking 'who am I?' beyond what you see and feel provides insights for inner and outer growth.

6. Recognising the potency of purpose over plan is wholeness.

7. Agency, breakthrough and clarity are interconnected.

Further reading

- Leadbeater, C (2016) *The Problem Solvers*. London: Pearson. [online] Available at: www.pearson. com/content/dam/corporate/global/pearson-dot-com/files/learning/Problem-Solvers-Web-.pdf (accessed 22 July 2024).

- University College London and Cardiff University (nd) School Transition and Adjustment Research Study (STARS). [online] Available at: www.ucl.ac.uk/pals/research/clinical-educational-and-health-psychology/research-groups/school-transition-and-adjustment (accessed 22 July 2024).

References

Brain & Life Magazine (2014) How Do Video Games Affect Brain Development in Children and Teens? [online] Available at: www.brainandlife.org/articles/how-do-video-games-affect-the-developing-brains-of-children (accessed 22 July 2024).

Chalkiadaki, A (2018) A Systematic Literature Review of 21st Century Skills and Competencies in Primary Education. *International Journal of Instruction*, 11(3): 1–16. [online] Available at: www. e-iji.net/dosyalar/iji_2018_3_1.pdf (accessed 22 July 2024).

Coe, R, Aloisi, C, Higgins, S and Elliot Major, L (2014) *What Makes Great Teaching?* The Sutton Trust. [online] Available at: www.suttontrust.com/wp-content/uploads/2014/10/What-Makes-Great-Teaching-REPORT.pdf (accessed 22 July 2024).

Devi, A (2020) *Essential Guides for Early Career Teachers: Special Educational Needs and Disability*. St Albans: Critical Publishing.

Draper, B (2011) *Spiritual Intelligence: A New Way of Being.* Oxford: Lion Books.

Evans, D, Borriello, G and Filed, A P (2018) A Review of the Academic and Psychological Impact of the Transition to Secondary Education. *Frontiers*, 9. https://doi.org/10.3389/fpsyg.2018.01482

Koepp, M J, Gunn, R N, Lawrence, A D, Cunningham, V J, Dagher, A, Jones, T, Brooks, D J, Bench, C J and Grasby, P M (1998) Evidence for Striatal Dopamine Release During a Video Game. *Nature*, 393: 266–8.

McGreal, S A (2017) What is 'Spiritual Intelligence' Anyway? *Psychology Today*, 6 September. [online] Available at: www.psychologytoday.com/us/blog/unique-everybody-else/201709/what-is-spiritual-intelligence-anyway (accessed 22 July 2024).

O'Sullivan, M, Brownsett, S and Copland, D (2019) Language and Language Disorders: Neuroscience to Clinical Practice. *Practical Neurology*, 19: 380–8.

Snape, R (2024) *The Curriculum Compendium*. London: Bloomsbury Publishing.

Speech and Language UK (2023) Listening to Unheard Children. [online] Available at: https://speechandlanguage.org.uk/listening-to-unheard-children (accessed 22 July 2024).

Waters, S, Lester, L and Cross, D (2014) How Does Support from Peers Compare with Support from Adults as Students Transition to Secondary School? *Journal of Adolescent Health*, 54: 543–9.

West, P, Sweeting, H and Young, R (2010) Transition Matters: Pupils' Experiences of the Primary–Secondary School Transition in the West of Scotland and Consequences for Well-Being and Attainment. *Research Papers in Education*, 25: 21–50.

Zeedyk, M S, Gallacher, J, Henderson, M, Hope, G, Husband, B and Lindsay, K (2003) Negotiating the Transition from Primary to Secondary School: Perceptions of Pupils, Parents and Teachers. *School Psychology International*, 24: 67–79.

Zohar, D and Marshall, I (2000) *SQ: Connecting with Our Spiritual Intelligence*. New York: Bloomsbury Publishing.

2 Abandonment or acceptance?

MARK STIBBE

Introduction

Everyone has a story; this is mine. My first traumatic experience of abandonment was when I was a baby. My birth mother left my twin sister and me at a home run by Anglican nuns in north London. The narrative from that point on played like an episode from the BBC's *Call the Midwife*. One of the sisters connected us with a couple who were looking for twins. A process of interviews and paperwork followed. At the age of seven months, my sister and I were both adopted by Philip and Joy Stibbe. This, at least in terms of our external circumstances, was a journey from abandonment to acceptance – abandonment by my birth mother (our biological father was not aware of our existence) and acceptance by our new adoptive family. Internally, the journey from *feeling* abandoned to *feeling* accepted was a much longer one. It was exacerbated after seven years when my adoptive parents chose to make me an early boarder.

I was sent away to a prep school on my eighth birthday. This was in some ways a more traumatic abandonment than the first one as a baby. Unlike then, I was this time conscious of what was going on in my world. I was all too aware of the ruptured attachment with my parents, my brother (my parents' biological son), my sister and my dog. I was also painfully conscious of the perilous nature of my new surroundings. I was beaten with a cane on my first night in front of the rest of my dormitory. I sobbed into my teddy bear. In the light of this cocktail of abandonment and abuse, it's no surprise that the journey to acceptance has been arduous.

That's my story.

What's yours?

After three decades of teaching and writing about that journey, I have come to realise that my story has a wider audience than simply boarding school survivors. I have listened to people in their twilight years telling me that my story speaks to their experience of being evacuated to unfamiliar homes in World War 2. I have had former foster children saying the same thing about being separated from a biological parent or parents and being placed in a new home. Ex-prisoners have told me they relate to my experience of being sent away to strange and scary institutions. I have also many times heard stories of children feeling abandoned within their own families. The deep wounds of abandonment, and the equally deep ache for acceptance, are not just things boarders and ex-boarders have to navigate. I see these same things in the eyes of children and young people in multiple contexts, including in the special school

I visit. Unless we make the journey from abandonment to acceptance, we are likely to remain forever bound by chains of shame and enslaved to toxic ways of soliciting the acceptance we crave.

Chapter aims ◎

My aim in this chapter is to describe how a person can make the journey from abandonment to acceptance. To do this, I will answer seven questions.

1. What is meant by abandonment?

2. What are the symptoms of abandonment?

3. What part does anger play?

4. What does acceptance look like?

5. What can we do to pivot from abandonment to acceptance?

6. What role does the brain play in our journey from abandonment to acceptance?

7. What contexts might facilitate this journey?

Reflection ⑦

This may be a helpful place to pause and look at your own life. To what extent are you still traumatised by experiences and feelings of abandonment? It has been said that 'hurting people end up hurting people'. If we are employed within, say, the worlds of education or therapy, and we ourselves have not yet made the journey from abandonment to acceptance, to what extent are we equipped to help people make that journey? If hurting people end up hurting people, liberated people end up liberating people. We can't give away what we haven't ourselves received. If we haven't found our own freedom, how can we set others free? On the other hand, if we have travelled our own hero's journey from abandonment to acceptance, we will be much better placed to function as a mentor to those yearning for their freedom.

So, where are you on this journey?

Application 🗒

My plan in this section is to try and answer the seven questions I posed earlier. The first was, '*What is meant by abandonment?*' There are two ways in which this word can be understood in this context. In the first, abandonment can be understood as an event or series of events. Abandonment in this sense is something that happens to a person. It can happen suddenly. Being orphaned is often traumatic precisely because it is dramatic. But it can also happen gradually and incrementally, over time. This is no less traumatic. Just because the abandonment occurs developmentally rather than in a moment doesn't lessen its severity or its impact.

The second way in which abandonment can be understood is as a feeling. If the first sense of the word is objective – that is, something external to you – the second sense is subjective. It is much more to do with the way you feel. Abandonment in this sense is the feeling of having been left alone or left behind. In my story, I was abandoned by my birth mother when she left my twin sister and me at a home for unmarried mums and babies in Hackney. I was abandoned a second time when I was sent away to boarding school on my eighth birthday. Both were events – things happening outside my control. These are both examples of abandonment in the first, more objective sense. But I came to *feel* abandoned as well. That took time in relation to my birth mother. I only connected with that traumatic feeling later in life when I was in my forties. But the feelings of abandonment I felt on the day I was left behind at boarding school were immediate, intense and immersive. I felt crushed by a sense of being alone. I didn't know who to trust. I didn't know where to turn for comfort. I didn't know what lay around the corner. I was afraid.

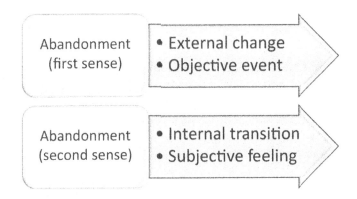

Figure 2.1 *Dimensions of abandonment*

As you look at Figure 2.1, ask yourself the questions, '*Do I know of anyone in my classroom who has experienced, or is experiencing, abandonment?*' '*Is there anyone who's feeling abandoned?*'

CASE STUDY 🔊

Miranda has a disagreement with her school friends on 16 March 2020. The date is significant because it is the day before the first lockdown in the UK, due to Covid-19. Miranda has done something silly that has annoyed her friends. She hopes that she will be able to patch things

→

up with them the following day at school. But that is not to be. Throughout lockdown, Miranda doesn't know if her friends have forgiven her. She feels alone. She doesn't speak to anyone at home about the turmoil she is experiencing. In any case, she can see her family members are preoccupied with adjusting to everyone being at home. In Miranda's heart and mind, the problem with her friends now gets bigger and bigger. She lives in fear of going back to school when the pandemic is over. The pain is excruciating. She considers ending it all. She starts self-harming to ease the pain. No one notices at first. She wears long sleeves and is always in trousers. But then summer comes and covering her scars becomes far more challenging. It takes Miranda a long time to recover and fully accept herself again, but with support and compassion she does. When she finally meets her friends at school to talk, none of them remember what happened on 16 March 2020. The challenges of lockdown have taken over their lives. They have had bigger problems to figure out, which is why they have been distant. They have been hurting too. Miranda learns that many of her friends' parents have lost their jobs; some are now having to access foodbank and other support services. Their lives have been turned upside down. They couldn't tell her at the time.

This leads to the second question: what are the symptoms of abandonment? What should we look for when it comes to the children we are looking after? What should we be alert to in our own lives if we've gone through the trauma of a ruptured attachment to a parent, parents or others?

The most common symptom of abandonment is fear. The person who has experienced abandonment both as an event and as an experience will often be weighed down by a deeply debilitating fear of future scenarios of broken attachment. The child or adult who has this trauma as part of their backstory may be driven by that fear into one of two patterns of behaviour. The first is **withdrawal**. Fearing further abandonment, the child or adult may opt out of all intimate relationships on the very reasonable grounds that they were disappointed before when their parent or parents left them alone/behind, so why wouldn't they be disappointed again by those who have a less invested reason for permanency?

CASE STUDY ⏻

Junior has had lots of friends in primary school, so when he moves to secondary school, he isn't worried. Year 7 turns out to be great, as most of the time he is still with his old friends. However, the transition to Year 8 is challenging. His friends have changed; they have new friends and new interests. Junior feels alone and scared. He starts to believe that no one likes him, that everyone is gossiping about him, and that he has been abandoned. He goes from being an A-grade student to not attending school at all. His SENCo now sets up 'a circle of friends'. This is a support group that scaffolds someone into making new friends. Junior is reluctant at first, but with so many absent marks on his record, he decides to give it a go. The 'circle of friends' programme enables Junior to be open and share what he has been feeling.

He soon realises that he, like his previous friends, has also changed. The intervention runs for about 15 weeks. Mirroring what has been happening in nature during that time, they talk about the changing seasons of life. This helps Junior to shift from feelings of abandonment to ones of hope. He figures he's going to enter and enjoy a new season – not the winter of abandonment (of *feeling* abandoned) but the bright summer months of acceptance (of *feeling* accepted). Some relationships have just been for a season, others for a reason.

The second behaviour that fear of abandonment can provoke in a child or an adult is what has been called **obsessive love** or relationship addiction (Forward, 2002). Frightened of losing someone they love, a person overinvests in intimate relationships. They become possessive to the point of suffocation. The person to whom they are attached becomes their fixation – the centre of their priorities, the goal of their existence. But this is not love at all. If love denies the other person their freedom, then it is based in narcissism not altruism. Obsessive love is often the wellspring for domestic abuse. It is an early stage in a recognisable process leading to the murder of a partner (Monkton Smith, 2022).

The number 1 symptom of abandonment – both as an event and as an experience – is therefore fear. Fear of being left alone/behind again. Fear of further severed attachments. Fear of more soul pain. This can lead to either isolation (withdrawal from relationships) or obsession (possessive relationships).

Is this something you see/have seen in the classroom? Is this something you see in your own story/life?

The third question is this: what part does anger play in abandonment? The answer is *a lot*. Keep in mind that there are signs as well as symptoms when it comes to abandonment (Stibbe, 2010). Symptoms are internal. You don't necessarily see them unless you're trained to discern them. Signs are external; they are visible and observable behaviours that require little coaching to spot. The person who has been abandoned may retreat into a cave of sadness, yes. Grief gets lodged deep within the human soul when a person is a victim of abandonment. This can be hidden. Anger, on the other hand, is a far less private phenomenon. It erupts like a volcano. When it comes from the abandoned person, it is often directed at the wrong person at the wrong time and in the wrong place.

Why does this happen? Let's say it's the mother who has abandoned the child. That child may start feeling intense anger towards their mother for leaving them behind/alone. This, over time, may start to turn from simmering to boiling, morphing in the process from anger to rage or what used to be called 'wrath'. Let's now say you are a female teacher in that child's world. One day, you do something that upsets the child. To you it seems trivial; to them it has been triggering. It has reminded them of their abandonment. What happens in this scenario? You are, in a sense, a mother figure in that child's world. You are an older, female role model. In military terms, you are a 'target-rich environment' for anyone suffering from maternal deprivation. When they start exhibiting rage with you, why is this happening? It's because they are getting angry with the wrong person in the wrong place at the wrong time. What is going on here is this: the child is attempting to hurt you. They may not mean to do it, but whether consciously or subconsciously, they are seeking to get you to feel for a moment what they live with all the time. They are trying to get you to feel what they feel. Abandoned.

CASE STUDY 🔊

Carlos is a bright boy. He has a good social circle and enjoys coming to school. However, all this changes when he turns eight. After he enters Year 4, his teacher notices him engaging in violent behaviour towards his peers – low level at first but growing in frequency. As his teacher, I become concerned. I invite his mother into school to discuss the matter. His mother tells me that at home Carlos has also started to become increasingly aggressive. She confides in me that her first husband was violent and that as a baby Carlos witnessed his mum being abused. Mum has since left her husband and has a new life. She thought Carlos had largely been unaffected by this, but my instinct is that Carlos is manifesting a repressed memory of trauma. Though he did not have the linguistic, cognitive or emotional development to fully understand what was happening, he still saw it. We decide it will be helpful for Carlos to go for counselling. We give him the option to have this in school or off site. He chooses off site. His mum is able and willing to take him. As his teacher, I tell him not to worry about his grades but to focus on his well-being. Within six months, Carlos is back to his lively, bubbly, kind self. I am also pleased to share that more than 20 years later, he has matured into a fine young man, taking responsibility for his life and enjoying a stable relationship.

Have you experienced this in the classroom from children with abandonment in their story? Have you experienced it in your relationships with significant adults? Are you yourself angry? Do you have anger management problems? Could it be that you're not angry with the right person? Do you need more emotional intelligence? Do you need to work at being emotionally healthy?

There really is only one antidote to this toxin of abandonment – acceptance. This leads me to the fourth question: what does acceptance look like? We are very used to hearing Brené Brown talking about shame as the feeling of being '*unworthy of love and belonging*' (Brown, 2015, p 58). That is a very helpful definition. The trauma of abandonment leads to the pain of shame.

What does shame look like? Shame is essentially an ontological word. It is about *being*. It is about who I think I am. It is to do with how much I think I'm worth. This is very different from guilt. Guilt is a functional word. It is to do with what I have done or what I am *doing*. When a person feels shame, they experience a deep-seated sense that they *are* defective, ugly, dirty. When a person feels guilty, they experience an equally deep-seated sense that they've *done* something defective, ugly, dirty. Shame circles like a vulture around who we think we are. Guilt claws at our memories of what we have done.

All this is immensely important when it comes to acceptance. Abandonment causes children to embrace shame – the feeling of being unworthy of love and belonging. They start believing the lie that if they had been less defective, ugly or dirty – less of a disappointment, maybe – then their parent(s) would not have left them behind or alone. What, then, is the opposite of abandonment? It is acceptance. What does acceptance look like? It looks like the opposite of shame. Honour is the gift of respect, time and empathy you give to another human being. When you honour a child in the classroom, you treat them as a human being of equal value to you, you give them the gift of your time – quality time, characterised by emotional engagement – and you listen attentively to what is going on in their emotional life, responding with 'unconditional positive regard' rather than aggression and judgement. This should be your default setting and mine; we model acceptance by giving the abandoned child the gift of honour. We say in our body language, our reactions, our words, our behaviour, *'You are worthy of love, and you are worthy of belonging here'.* Whenever we do this, we help that child a little bit further on the journey from abandonment to acceptance.

Is this your default setting?

Reflection ⑦

»   Re-read Miranda's story from earlier in the chapter. What are you seeing and understanding now in a deeper way that you didn't notice before?

So, what can we do to pivot from abandonment to acceptance? This is the fifth question. I could write an entire book on this subject, especially since it's a much-neglected topic. The answer, I believe, lies in the art of forgiving – maybe a lost art in our cancel culture. No one is pretending that forgiveness is easy. It took me many years before I was able to forgive my birth mother for leaving my twin sister and me in Hackney. It took me many more years before I was able to forgive my adoptive parents for adding to this trauma by leaving me at boarding school – a *second orphaning*, as I call it (Stibbe, 2021, pp 47–8).

Forgiveness should be described more than prescribed, narrated more than mandated, on the therapeutic journey. The fracturing of critical attachments leaves lasting scars in the souls of those who are victims of it. One of the pathways towards forgiveness involves the healing power of empathy. The French have a proverb – *'to understand all is to forgive all'*. In other words, when you begin to understand better the person who abandoned you, you are in a much stronger position when it comes to forgiving them, even though it can be challenging.

Let's take an example. In the case of my birth mother, I had something of an epiphany when my adoptive mother decided to pass something on to me. I was in my forties at the time. The item in question was a letter written to her by my birth mother on my (and Claire's) first birthday. In the letter, my birth mother expressed the pain she had felt giving us up for what would end up being an adoption. She spoke about why she had made this difficult decision. That solitary handwritten letter gave me the grace I needed to forgive her. In understanding better why she had done what she did, I was able to release her from my bitterness. Forgiving her, I was able to pivot from abandonment to acceptance – including self-acceptance.

Forgiveness is therefore a critical and often neglected stage in the therapeutic journey. When we have truly forgiven those who abandoned us, we know for sure that our forgiveness is total and effective by virtue of this one telling fact: when we remember our abandonment, we no longer recall it with a wince of pain. We remember it without the strong emotions of resentment and rage that accompanied and characterised our former recollections.

One word of warning though. Forgiveness does not necessarily mean reconciliation. You may have received considerable healing through forgiving the one who abandoned you, but the one who abandoned you may have experienced no such advances in discovery and wholeness. If that person has an abusive temperament, it would be unwise to go back into their world and offer the hand of friendship. Until they have shown genuine remorse for what they did to you, and been through therapy, they may not be trustworthy, let alone safe, for you to reconnect with.

This is why forgiveness requires wisdom. It requires us to be wise about what we do *after* we forgive those who have traumatised us. But it also requires wisdom about how we understand the importance of this act *before* we do it. Before we forgive, we need to recognise that the most important reason for doing this is our own liberation. While we remain bitter and resentful, we embrace the false belief that we are keeping that person in the prison of our anger. But it is not the offenders who are imprisoned. It is us. When we forgive others, it is not the case that they are freed. It is the case that we are set free. This is why the famous statement by Nelson Mandela in *The Long Walk to Freedom* rings so true and is cited by so many: '*As I walked out the door toward the gate that would lead to my freedom, I knew if I didn't leave my bitterness and hatred behind, I'd still be in prison.*'

So, my questions to you are these. Firstly, is there anyone who has abandoned you that you need to forgive? This is vital. You cannot model to others – for example, children in your classroom – what you have not yourself lived.

Secondly, if you have a testimony of forgiveness, how are you going to harness its positive energy to help sufferers of abandonment to make their own transition from victim to victor?

This leads me to the sixth question. What role does the brain play in our journey from abandonment to acceptance? This is an important question because in counselling there has been a great emphasis in recent decades on the *cognitive* pathway to healing. This often consists of training the brain to believe positive rather than negative things about your life. The basis for this is the discovery that the human brain is neuroplastic, and that it is this very plasticity which enables us to learn new ways of perceiving reality. However, this is helpful only to a degree. To understand why, have a look at the cycle in Figure 2.2.

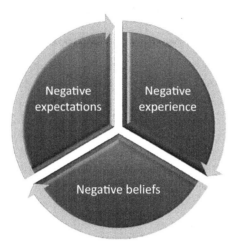

Figure 2.2 *Negative experience, beliefs and expectations in the cycle of abandonment*

If a person experiences abandonment, this is a negative experience. It is an injurious, traumatic experience of separation. This in turn leads a person to embrace negative beliefs. '*I was not worthy of being loved by my father.*' '*I was not worthy of belonging at home with my mother.*' These sorts of toxic thoughts lead to negative expectations. These are often couched in statements involving the words 'always' and 'never'. '*I will* never *be able to trust anyone not to abandon me in the future.*' '*I will* always *be abandoned by those I love.*' In cognitive approaches to therapy, the client is encouraged and empowered to replace negative beliefs with positive ones. The neuroplastic brain, they contend, does the rest.

From my experience of helping people with abandonment issues, I would argue that we need to start the healing process further back. We need to start with the negative experience. Before negative beliefs can be replaced by positive ones, the negative experience of abandonment needs to be countered by a positive experience of acceptance, care, compassion and so on.

Figure 2.3 *Positive experience, beliefs and expectations in the cycle of acceptance*

Put in neuroscientific terms, the limbic system needs to be enlisted in the healing process, not just the neocortex. Let me explain.

The exercise of replacing negative beliefs with positive ones is an exercise involving the frontal cortex. This is the part of our brain where we reason, analyse, reflect and so on. Using this logic centre, we attempt to harness the neuroplasticity of the brain to change our thinking. But is this enough? My thesis is that the limbic system or feeling centre of the brain needs to be activated before the neocortex can work effectively. In other words, something *affective* needs to precede the *cognitive*. A positive experience needs to *displace* the negative experience before positive beliefs can *replace* negative ones. In other words, love, not just logic, needs to be involved in the healing process. Trauma is just too powerful for logic alone to remove its central and controlling power. Love must precede logic, whether that love is divine (in the form of a mystical experience) or human. The release of oxytocin (the bonding chemical) leads to the release of dopamine (the feel-good chemical). Love is not love without bonding.

The brain is therefore immensely important although much more of its seemingly infinite capacities need to be utilised. The neocortex is vital, yes, but only if its cognitive operations flow out of something affective in the limbic system – something that has the power to displace a negative experience and lead to the reset of the neuroplastic brain. That something is the acceptance that derives from love. When an abandoned child encounters a love that is safe, they have a chance of moving from abandonment to acceptance, from fear to security. This all therefore starts with the positive experience of love. This, in turn, leads to positive beliefs ('*I am worthy of giving and receiving love*') and positive expectations ('*I will never be alone*'). The question for those who care for children with abandonment issues is this: are you prepared to be vehicles of love?

This moves us on to my final question: what contexts might facilitate such a therapeutic journey? The obvious answer is 'safe spaces'. I have already used the word 'safe' in the last paragraph in the context of love. The love offered by counsellors and teachers needs to be safe. It needs to be utterly trustworthy, accepting and calm. In other words, it needs to be the opposite of oppressive and abusive (which would automatically disqualify this state of being from being deserving of the word 'love'). I have seen with my own eyes the most amazing human beings manifesting this kind of love – teachers and teaching assistants in the classrooms of special schools, for example. I have watched such unsung heroes listen to the rage of an abandoned child without judgement, harshness, resentment or aggression. I have seen them absorb this anger like a miraculous sponge. I have seen them refuse to walk away and instead stay present to the child, listening empathetically, filling that child's virtually empty 'love tank' with a gallon or two of extreme and extraordinary acceptance.

And here's the thing. Often these staff members are so excellent at doing this because they have gone through abandonment themselves, and they either wished for what they are offering these children or were blessed enough to receive it, and they've learned – to use a film title – to 'pay it forward'.

Those who embody and display this kind of love not only provide safe spaces. They *are* safe spaces – safe spaces for dealing with dangerous issues. So, my question now is this: are you a safe space?

A 'safe space' is another word for 'home'. What you're doing when you create such mobile, flexible, safe spaces is this: you are facilitating one of the most deeply healing human experiences – homecoming.

Key takeaway

That final thought leads me to quote one of my favourite authors in the field of attachment theory, Dan Hughes. He has said this about the word 'home' and the connotation of safety.

> *Your home is your secure base. When the world has become too stressful or too stimulating, or when you have just been away too long, your home finds its way into your mind and body and back you come to repair, rejuvenate, and recharge. You return home if you are able, and if you cannot return home, thinking about it comforts you.*
>
> (Hughes, 2009, p 76)

Key question

» Are you able to replicate the positive experience of homecoming by offering a safe and accepting space for the children you serve – especially those who have been through ruptured attachment and abandonment?

Call to action

In all of this, remember your agency, especially if you yourself have been through the trauma of abandonment. You can take responsibility for your own journey of healing so that you can become a mentor to those who are still living in the land of trauma. In other words, you can give away what you have learned.

Classrooms need to be filled with mentors who have made or who are making this therapeutic journey so that they can give young people one of the most precious gifts of all – their wisdom. Remember, wisdom is not the same as knowledge. Knowledge tells you *what*. Wisdom tells you *how*.

Children need to know how to make their own hero's journey out of the prison of abandonment into the landscape of acceptance. No other lesson they could learn in the classroom could ever prove more lifechanging than that.

And I leave you with this thought: in the future, education needs to give as much attention and value to the healing of hearts as it does to the filling of minds.

Editors' note

Due to the sensitive and personal nature of this topic (abandonment or acceptance), Mark has structured this chapter slightly differently from the rest. We encourage you to re-read the chapter and copy and complete the 'Reflection' table below, adding in where you notice **agency, breakthrough** and **clarity on personal identity**. These three core constructs form the central structure of this book (see Chapter 1).

Reflection ⑦

Copy out the table below and complete it in as much detail as possible.

	Agency	Breakthrough	Clarity on personal identity
Comments from this chapter			
Implications for my classroom			

References

Brown, B (2015) *Daring Greatly*. New York: Penguin Life.

Forward, S (2002) *Obsessive Love: When It Hurts Too Much to Let Go*. Reprint edition. New York: Random House Publishing Group.

Hughes, D A (2009) *Principles of Attachment-Focused Parenting: Effective Strategies to Care for Children*. New York: W W Norton & Co.

Monkton Smith, J (2022) *In Control: Dangerous Relationships and How They End in Murder*. London: Bloomsbury.

Stibbe, M (2010) *I Am Your Father: What Every Heart Needs to Know*. Oxford: Monarch.

Stibbe, M (2021) *Home at Last: Freedom from Boarding School Pain*. 2nd ed. Milton Keynes: Malcolm Down Publishing Ltd.

3 Rejection or rewiring?

ANITA DEVI AND SUE JAGGER

Introduction

As we grow, we become more aware of who we are, what we believe and what we value. We can take responsibility for our decisions and actions, for the language we choose and the way we present ourselves. We can explain to others what engages us, how we learn best and what our goals are. We have agency, which enables us to have resilience: both internal and external resilience. As classroom teachers, it is important to realise that all our students have agency too. We need to be aware that our students are individuals who can communicate their likes, dislikes and preferences for learning styles and how they can best be supported. It is through this agency that students can become more resilient, which will enable them to deal with the situations and challenges that they meet. Agency is created through emotions, thoughts and feelings.

Emotions, thoughts and feelings matter. They form the basis of what we say and do, which form our character. There is a circular connectivity to this, such that we often miss the starting point of personal identity.

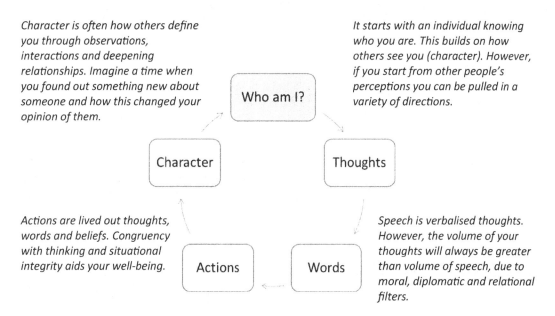

Character is often how others define you through observations, interactions and deepening relationships. Imagine a time when you found out something new about someone and how this changed your opinion of them.

It starts with an individual knowing who you are. This builds on how others see you (character). However, if you start from other people's perceptions you can be pulled in a variety of directions.

Actions are lived out thoughts, words and beliefs. Congruency with thinking and situational integrity aids your well-being.

Speech is verbalised thoughts. However, the volume of your thoughts will always be greater than volume of speech, due to moral, diplomatic and relational filters.

Figure 3.1 *Cyclical connection between identity, thoughts, words, actions and character*

Emotions, thoughts and feelings can help or hinder our growth. In everyday conversations, we can use these words interchangeably, but in reality, they are quite distinctive experiences and processes.

- A thought is the action or process of the mind. It is usually structured through an idea or opinion and is the byproduct of incoming stimuli from the senses. A thought can be sudden and/or a slow maturation process over time.

- A feeling is part mental and part physical response marked by pleasure, pain, attraction or repulsion. A feeling signals the existence of a response but does not necessarily define the nature and intensity of it.

- Emotion is the indication of excitement or agitation. It is the expression of the feeling, and like feelings it can encompass both the positive and the negative.

Chapter aims ◎

This chapter addresses seven questions around the three core themes of this book.

1. How do you choose what influences your thoughts?
2. Does intentionally choosing a focus help or hinder?
3. Why is to fight one of the three impulsive responses for students?
4. Does flight work?
5. Is freeze a healthy state?
6. What triggers self-awareness?
7. How can relationships help to rewire rejection?

Activate agency

1. How do you choose what influences your thoughts?

We take in information through our senses. Durie (2005) refers to the senses as '*doors of perception*'. Different researchers catalogue how many senses humans have through different numerical values. For example, the website for the American not-for-profit Twenty-One Senses (nd) makes a case for both 21 distinct senses and eight sensory systems. Devi (2020) refers to 33 senses and seven key ones used in the classroom. You can read Chapter 7 of this book for a further discussion on this.

The agency element to consider here falls into three categories.

a. Filter system of what comes in

Some of your senses have a one-way system, eg the ear hears and the mouth speaks. But the tongue tastes and is involved in speech production. Likewise, your eyes see and communicate, as part of the non-verbal schema. So, applying a filter on incoming information is critical, especially in a world where information overload is prevalent, being online is the norm and the fast economy determines the pace of change.

Scrolling online results in data gathering by producers and marketers, which through algorithms affects subsequent content exposure. However, humans need to apply their own filter and intentionality about what information is taken in and processed.

In historic computer speak, this was known as GIGO – garbage in, garbage out.

b. Filter system of what goes out

What you say (literal or non-verbal) and what you do affect others around you. So again, there is a need to be intentional. Your core character values, such as kindness, being polite, non-violent, calm, will often determine this.

c. Integration of sensory information

Whether you operate from eight sensory systems, or 21 or 33 senses, your senses are simultaneously receiving and giving information. Most of us never learnt this; we developed the skill through trial and error and activities such as playing on swings, slides and roundabouts. For some, this has not been learnt or experienced and so they experience sensory overload.

2.   Does intentionally choosing a focus help or hinder?

The best way to answer this is through experimentation.

Application

 »   Stand in the middle of a classroom, turn around 360 degrees at a reasonable pace and make a note of what you see. Now try the same activity, but only focus on items that are green or square, etc.

When leading this activity in a workshop, most people share that by focusing on less, they actually notice more.

The opposite can also be true. Think of the child in the classroom whose attention and interest are only focused on one thing, such as trains. This often comes at the expense of missing out on other useful information and learning.

The key here is not one thing or another, but a personalised balance with a view to stretch and learn more as part of the life transformational process. The word balance is vital for your thoughts, feelings, emotions and actions.

> # Reflection ⑦
>
> »   As a teacher/practitioner, how do you model balance in the classroom?
>
> »   How do you encourage your learners to adopt a balanced view/stance?
>
> »   How does balance permeate both the formal curriculum and the informal culture/well-being of your learning environment?

Breakthrough

Emotions, thoughts and feelings lead to our impulsive responses. For example, if someone walks past me when I am out for a walk and says '*Hello*', my natural impulse response is to smile and reply '*Hello*'. Some impulse responses can lead students, particularly neurodiverse students, to impulsive responses such as fight, flight or freeze. This is usually in response to a situation which makes them feel vulnerable because they have become overwhelmed. However, experiencing something like fight, flight or freeze can lead a student to a clarity of self-awareness through the learning experience that takes place. The student develops further clarity in understanding themselves, gaining strength from their experiences.

3.   Why is to fight one of the three impulsive responses for students?

The way a teacher reacts to a student's impulsive response is crucial. On one occasion, I can remember a student entering my classroom and being incredibly angry; they were shouting across the classroom that I was a liar, and it was all my fault. The emotions that the student was displaying were intense and I had no idea about what they were referring to as the student was in 'fight' mode. Something had happened earlier in the school day, and they felt that I was responsible for creating a negative perception of them. I had not actually been involved at all, nor did I have any awareness of the event and the student had misunderstood a communication from another member of staff. I highlight this situation because the student decided to isolate themselves as an emotive response to a situation, making themselves vulnerable. They were not able at that moment in time to control their feelings or response; they were in 'fight' mode. This was due to the fear that they felt of being accused of something for which they felt they were not responsible. The next lesson was totally different. The student was calm and engaged and applied themselves well to the learning. This was because we talked between the lessons and were able to understand one another's perspectives. I shared with the student how their actions made me feel while reinforcing our expectations of a respectful relationship, and they were able to calmly share why they had felt angry. The conversation was an opportunity for me as a teacher to model effective choice of behaviour and for the student to reflect upon their response and choice. The student's emotional vulnerability had led them to a path of fight, but their reflections enabled them to learn from the event.

4.   Does flight work?

Flight is a natural response. If we are fearful and therefore vulnerable in a situation that we find ourselves in, we would naturally want to leave. However, through flight we can become isolated, we might leave in a hurry, not think about where we are going and therefore end up alone, further away than we had originally imagined or, in the worst-case scenario, lost. However, the action of flight itself, the physicality of running away, might aid our overload; it might provide us with time and space to think and reflect. As a young classroom teacher, I can remember making the mistake of running after a student who had chosen to leave the classroom. As a more experienced teacher, I now realise that running after a student in this manner is not necessary; they are in school – most importantly, they are safe and cannot go very far. They will at some point return, and more often than not the very act of leaving the initial environment provides them with an opportunity to think about how they have chosen to interact, and maybe how they could better respond to the situation.

I have seen how flight can be beneficial to a student, particularly if they are neurodiverse. On one occasion, a student had received a detention slip and instead of going to the detention to discuss the situation with the teacher they sought to find me. They were anxious about attending the detention for several reasons: they didn't like entering a classroom if they didn't know where everyone was sitting; they thought that they would have to explain themselves to the teacher in front of others, something which they did not feel comfortable with, and they felt out of control. The student therefore felt vulnerable and decided to find a way out, so they left the situation behind and tried to avoid it instead. When the student spoke with me, I could see that their thoughts were '*if I don't attend this detention, I am in control; it is my decision*'. It was only through us having a conversation away from the initial environment that the student could begin to see that the easier, more straightforward route would be to go to the detention and quietly talk to the teacher. Flight had provided the student with the time and space to reflect, which led to a positive outcome: the student was empowered to realise that they could respond in a different manner should this situation arise again.

5.   Is freeze a healthy state?

Imagine if you are in a busy shop in London on a Saturday morning before Christmas. The shop is full of people all talking, walking and looking around searching for their next purchase, a real cacophony for the senses. To a neurodiverse person this can be immensely challenging as it can be overwhelming for the senses and can result in an impulsive response. A response such as freezing and not moving, just as my daughter did. However, she has the internal resilience to be able to move through this response; without physically moving, she said, '*Don't tell me I have sensory overload*'. I just left her for a few moments. As a mum it was a moment of fear, considering what might happen next, but it was also immensely enlightening: I could see that she was able to cope with this situation should it happen again. It is the type of moment that provided her with the ability to make connections and to learn, a point of reference for her in the future that she will return to should she feel sensorially overwhelmed again in a similar environment.

Clarity on personal identity

6. What triggers self-awareness?

About two decades ago, Anita was given a central government research grant to test the impact of 'stillness' on academic progress (Devi, 2002). Every day in maths (which was always after morning break time), eight-year-olds were led through different stillness activities that lasted no more than five minutes at the start of the lesson. Stillness is different to mindfulness. The activities were varied and included counting the 'sound' of objects, holding musical notes, counting breaths, counting time, visualisations and other breathing activities. Social media wasn't as prevalent back then, but airwave and airtime noise were. The year group consisting of 60 pupils were mixed ability, from deprived backgrounds and many with severe special educational needs. At the end of the year, three main findings emerged.

1. The value-added data of pupils in mathematics increased significantly.

2. The pupils' language and use of vocabulary was extended to affect both speaking and writing. Many pupils actually taught their parents and family at home.

3. The pupils experienced self-awareness and this enhanced their self-regulation. Most notably, friendships and teamwork increased and conflicts in the playground reduced.

And finally:

7. How can relationships help to rewire rejection?

John Hattie in his book *Visible Learning* (2017) identifies *'collective teacher efficacy'* as the most effective factor that influences student achievement. I find this extremely interesting because at the centre of a classroom culture is the teacher–student relationship – it creates the culture through which the student will become engaged in learning and achieve their best.

> *When leaders have a pulse on the emotional tone of the team, they can anticipate pitfalls that might occur during collaboration, sense when tensions rise, and not only have the fortitude to address the issues but do so in a way that is respectful to the feelings and viewpoints of others.*
>
> (Donohoo et al, 2018)

This concept mirrors the relationships within a classroom. If the relationships between the students and the teacher, students and their peers, learning support assistant and students, are positive then the members of the classroom community will have the agency to identify challenges and work through them to ensure that their shared goals of high expectations and high achievement are effective. Neurodiverse students are impulsive, *'predictably unpredictable'*, and therefore there will be occasions when there are challenges to overcome. However, the key to ensuring that the challenges become opportunities to learn relies upon the relationships at their centre.

Key takeaways 📖

»   As a classroom teacher, how do you model good relationships in the classroom?

»   How do you encourage your students to interact with one another?

»   How do you encourage your students to reflect upon their often-impulsive responses to a situation?

Further reading

• Devi, A (2020) *Essential Guides for Early Career Teachers: Special Educational Needs and Disability.* St Albans: Critical Publishing.

References

Devi, A (2002) It's All in the Mind! Paper delivered at the 9th Annual International Conference on *Education, Spirituality and the Whole Child*, 20–22 June 2002, University of Surrey, Roehampton.

Devi, A (2020) *Essential Guides for Early Career Teachers: Special Educational Needs and Disability.* St Albans: Critical Publishing.

Donohoo, J, Hattie, J and Eells, R (2018) *The Power of Collective Efficacy.* ASCD. [online] Available at: www.ascd.org/el/articles/the-power-of-collective-efficacy (accessed 22 July 2024).

Durie, B (2005) Senses Special: Doors of Perception. *New Scientist*, 26 January. [online] Available at: www.newscientist.com/article/mg18524841-600-senses-special-doors-of-perception (accessed 22 July 2024).

Hattie, J (2017) Hattie Ranking: 252 Influences and Effect Sizes Related to Student Achievement. *Visible Learning.* [online] Available at: https://visible-learning.org/hattie-ranking-influences-effect-sizes-learning-achievement (accessed 22 July 2024).

Twenty-One Senses (nd) [online] Available at: www.twentyonesenses.org/about-the-senses (accessed 22 July 2024).

4 Learning or labels?

SARAH MOSELEY

Introduction

In the story *The Star Thrower* (1978), Loren Eiseley describes a scenario where an individual on the beach makes progress by focusing on one starfish to make a wider impact on the whole community. Enabling the one starfish is seen as progress towards a greater good. This story has profoundly affected my own professional practice and ethos in the classroom. The individual in this story can be either a child (ie a learner) or an adult (ie an educator).

In the world of education, at times we can become overwhelmed by the enormity of the task and the increasing number and diversity of needs we see in the classroom. Therefore, too often, the relationship between 'learning' and 'labels of need' profoundly shapes the experiences of both educators and learners. This can be both a positive and negative dynamic. Positively, a label gives the educator clues as to how to support this learner. However, adversely, your perception of the 'label' may hinder their achievement.

Attainment is the standards learners demonstrate in line with any national curriculum. Achievement is about personal growth and aspiration. This can be both small steps and giant leaps.

This chapter offers insights and practical strategies to both educators and families, fostering an inclusive and supportive educational journey for all learners. Through targeted and frequent stimulation, such as engaging in new and challenging activities, the brain can create new connections and pathways, which can improve learning outcomes. Furthermore, consistent and structured learning experiences can help strengthen these connections and make them more efficient. In particular, I focus on how to extend reading, as this is the basis for writing and wider curriculum engagement. Children move from presented and printed text to creating their own recorded ideas, and, in many ways, oracy and spelling becomes the bridge between reading and writing.

Chapter aims ◎

Using the ABC framework of agency, breakthrough and clarity that is the golden thread running through this book, I seek to address seven questions.

Activate agency

1.   How do educators use observed patterns of behaviour and/or 'labels' to enhance professional curiosity without making assumptions?

2.   How can educators create a culture that fosters ownership and responsibility of the learner/s?

Breakthrough

3.   How can educators use targeted stimuli to promote good outcomes for all?

4.   In the classroom, how can stretch and failure accelerate the learning breakthrough?

Clarity on personal identity

5.   How can educators support learners to know that they are communicators of their own thoughts?

6.   What practices can be employed in the classroom (and wider setting) to encourage learners to celebrate their talents and move beyond labels?

And finally, in exploring the broader principles of Universal Design for Learning (UDL), I ask:

7.   Is a label-free but highly inclusive learning environment possible?

Activate agency

Neurodiversity challenges the traditional medical model that views neurological differences as deficits or disorders that need to be fixed or normalised. Instead, it recognises that individuals with different neurotypes possess unique abilities and perspectives, making unique contributions to society. Just as biodiversity is essential for a thriving ecosystem, neurodiversity enriches the social fabric and enhances the collective intelligence of our communities. As educators you need the tools to navigate the complexity of today's classrooms, starting with recognising that each learner brings unique needs and strengths to the learning environment and that these are not fixed. The nature of human design allows for continual growth and refinement.

Inclusion begins with a deep understanding of the diverse needs, strengths and abilities of our learners. As educators, our role is to build children and young people's learning capacity by encouraging agency, ownership and curiosity (Swann, 2012). To do this you must consider what the barriers to learning may be and how you can go beyond the restricted view of labels to create effective connections to empower our learners. Instead of assuming that a label defines a learner's capabilities or limitations, educators can use it as a starting point for understanding the individual's unique needs and strengths to ensure ongoing progress. This involves gathering and using information gained through observations, assessments and dialogue with learners, their families and other professionals involved. It should be noted that often information gathered from various sources may 'appear' to contradict other information.

Educators are like detectives, deciphering the intricate patterns of behaviour exhibited by learners. If we begin with the similarities between our learners rather than the differences, we can build on the strengths of our class. This shift allows educators to move beyond the limitations of diagnosis and instead develop a more curious capacity to the learning approach. In my work I'm often asked where to begin with learners who are struggling or reluctant to read. My first response is to ask educators what is it that learners enjoy doing? What currently motivates or engages them, gives them that zing, encourages them to focus or contribute to activities within the classroom or in the home environment? These are essential windows of information that should be used to provide engaging learning opportunities to build new skills. The foundation of this is knowing your learners.

Reflection ⑦

»   Take a moment to consider your classroom and those learners who may struggle with specific aspects of literacy.

»   What do you know about their strengths and things that they enjoy?

CASE STUDY ⊕

In a Year 3 primary classroom, a student named David was frequently labelled as 'disruptive' due to his behaviour. This initially led to a number of strategies being put into place to correct this. However, this leads to much more challenging behaviour being seen. When David moved to Year 4, his new teacher spent time with David, beginning to gather more information about what might be at the root of the challenges exhibited. The behaviour was observed primarily during certain activities or transitions within the classroom. Through observations and discussions with David's family and other professionals, the educator gained valuable insights into David's behaviour patterns. It became evident that David's behaviour was linked to sensory overload, particularly in noisy or crowded environments. Targeted interventions to support David's sensory needs were put into place, including making the classroom environment more predictable, implementing sensory breaks and providing noise-cancelling headphones.

The implementation of these changes had a significant impact on David's behaviour and overall well-being. By addressing his sensory needs, David's disruptive behaviour diminished, and he became more engaged and participative in classroom activities. Furthermore, regular reviews and discussions with David helped reinforce his understanding

→

of his sensory needs, empowering him to advocate for himself effectively. If we change our perspective from seeing behaviours as something that we need to change to viewing them as something that will provide us with an opportunity to connect with the child, there is a shift in what we may do next. We will meet the child where they are, rather than where we would want them to be.

Reflection ⑦

» How might this case study challenge your current perceptions of disruptive behaviour in the classroom, and what steps could you take to better support learners in your own educational setting?

Begin with changing our perceptions

It is fundamental that rather than searching for a change in your learners, you turn the focus back on yourself as a practitioner (Dix, 2017). Your focus is to ensure progress and growth for your learners by being open to change yourself. This is both the joy and tension of teaching. If you perceive a situation in a limited way, you may only consider one specific approach. You may be quick to use labels and diagnoses which lead us to make assumptions and use stereotypes. For example, if you see certain behaviours as problems or difficulties, it does not encourage you to start from where the learner is currently at. You may not consider the stage or schema a learner is working within as a reason for repetitive behaviours or patterns of play. These are essential to the development of higher cognitive skills and could be built on to consolidate further learning.

CASE STUDY 🔊

Samantha, a Year 2 learner, spent a great deal of time playing games which involved throwing, dropping or rolling. This made it difficult to engage her in more structured literacy teaching. The teacher had some understanding of schema theory (Vygotsky, 2004) and realised Samatha was working within the Trajectory Schema. The teacher planned literacy activities which involved games where throwing, rolling or dropping are built into the structure. The aim was to harness her natural instincts and engage her in learning built on her likes and strengths (Athey, 2007). The teacher used targets, sponges, balls, large dice and more to create access to literacy and develop an understanding of text. The impact was that Samatha was able to engage and complete activities with greater confidence.

This positive way of reflecting on the behaviour of the learner as opposed to stopping it enables learners to be supported through celebrating their strengths.

The language of inclusion is changing, and we are repositioning children with special educational needs from problems back to learners (Heiskanen, 2018).

Reflection ⑦

» Consider how fostering an understanding of behaviour through schema theory contributes positively to learning opportunities compared to the potentially limiting effects of using labels (see 'Nutbrown' in Further reading list).

A commonly used label is that of dyslexia. While this label may highlight challenges related to reading and language processing, it doesn't encapsulate the entirety of the learner's abilities. It creates a view that all learners with dyslexia are the same, yet we know that every learner is unique, and that developmental stages, the environment and emotional states also impact on learning. A learner labelled as dyslexic might possess exceptional creativity, problem-solving skills or a remarkable aptitude for visual thinking. These strengths could be a way to support and engage them in learning opportunities.

It is crucial to be aware that any label, when used to define or describe the needs of a learner, can lead to unconscious pedagogical decisions that impact on the future outcomes of all.

> Whatever role we have, we all implicitly act as pedagogical gatekeepers and so, at every point of decision-making, we should all be asking ourselves, 'What aspects of pedagogy (supporting learning) is this decision encouraging, influencing or preventing?'.
>
> (Aubrey-Smith, 2023)

During my career, I found that some labels also topped others, for example, labels such as severe or moderate learning difficulties were used to define many difficulties, including literacy needs. A more inclusive approach would be to have a toolkit of supportive strategies that can be used for specific literacy needs.

CASE STUDY 🔊

A toolkit of approaches

James faced challenges in literacy, including reading and writing. After recent training around specific literacy difficulties, the class teacher recognised the overlap in cognitive processes between dyslexia and moderate learning difficulties. To address James' needs, she decided to implement dyslexia-informed strategies, including multisensory and structured approaches tailored to improve literacy skills. These were based on James' interests, which included superheroes and super cars. These strategies significantly enhanced James' literacy skills and confidence. Through multisensory techniques and structured instruction (including writing his own books using images of supercars), he improved reading fluency and comprehension. The tailored approach alleviated his frustration, leading to a positive shift in his attitude towards learning. This led to him engaging more positively with literacy and print-based tasks.

Application

» **Embed multisensory instruction:** Engage multiple senses (sight, sound, touch, movement) to motivate and bring the fun back into learning, providing opportunities to link oral language and print (Moseley, 2023) (see Chapter 7).

» **Incorporate structured literacy approach**: Scaffold instruction to provide additional support and repetition as needed, gradually increasing the complexity of tasks as learners progress. Scaffolded templates and different structures for recording are useful for this.

» **Integrate assistive technology:** Provide access to text-to-speech software, speech-to-text tools and word prediction programs to assist with reading, writing and spelling tasks. Use audiobooks, digital texts and multimedia resources to provide alternative formats for presenting information and opportunities for repetition with engagement.

For many learners, being labelled with a specific condition can inadvertently create a self-fulfilling prophecy shaping their beliefs about their capabilities. It can affect their self-esteem, confidence and motivation, impacting on their understanding of what they can do to reduce their own barriers to learning. Learners need to feel empowered; unfortunately, being labelled solely by a condition can lead to a sense of inadequacy and self-doubt. These labels may inadvertently reinforce negative stereotypes, creating barriers to acceptance and understanding. For example, if a learner knows that they are labelled as 'disruptive', they may act in a way that is in line with the label. Or they may feel they have no power or agency to change this perception of others.

Creating a classroom culture that fosters ownership and responsibility among learners is essential for their growth and engagement. You can create a culture of autonomy and responsibility by involving learners in goal setting, decision-making and self-assessment processes. Providing opportunities to reflect on progress, identify areas for growth and take proactive steps towards achieving their goals cultivates a sense of ownership and accountability. This demonstrates your belief in learners and their learning capacity.

Breakthrough

As educators you must also develop your understanding of neuroplasticity and use it to maximise the brain's ability to change in response to experience. If you understand how the experiences you provide or create determine what enters the brain and how the brain processes this information, you can see the pivotal role you play in the learning process. Educators can harness the principles of neuroplasticity to create optimal learning environments that promote cognitive development and positive outcomes for all learners.

Historically for learners who struggle with specific aspects of learning, there has been a tendency to give them more of the same, supporting these deficits through repetition. Research has demonstrated that we are not hardwired to learn to read; we must learn and make connections in our brains through repeated exposure to literacy (Wolf, 2008). The neuroplasticity of the brain's connections and circuits will link and change in response to interactions with the environments (Wolf, 2008). We know that if we increase varied repetition and frequency, connections in our brains are strengthened, helping to build muscle memory. This supports information to be retained and therefore moved to the learner's long-term memory (Gathercole, 2008). Due to this complex neurological and neurophysiological process, learners need to enjoy words again and again in different contexts to deepen their understanding. We need to ensure that these rich repeated experiences are accessible, meaningful and engaging for all learners.

When you read aloud with a child, it leads to changes in the brain. As they hear the language read, neurons are activated, creating new circuits and stronger connections. Targeted and frequent stimulation through exposure to nursery rhymes, sound activities, songs and poems has been found to be particularity effective for developing and strengthening literacy skills (Ehri, 2001). The processing of these phonetic patterns and word connections during rhyme engagement reinforces neural pathways dedicated to language processing. The rhythmic and repetitive nature of rhymes provides a steady stream of stimulation, facilitating the creation of fresh neural connections and fortifying existing ones. With repeated exposure, the brain undergoes refinement in its language processing capabilities, leading to the development of foundation skills required to become a reader.

CASE STUDY ⊛

The power of rhyme to build connections

Emily was seven and loved songs and nursey rhymes, often repeating them while playing, but she was reluctant to engage with any books or reading activities. Her teacher understood the connection between rhymes and the brain's ability to strengthen connections required for language and literacy development. She picked fun rhymes that Emily liked and used them in learning activities. They played with words, rhythm and repetition to make learning enjoyable and engaging. They began to use speech to text to make her own songs and rhymes. This helped to stimulate neural pathways dedicated to language processing. The outcome was that Emily started to engage with print; she began to read and understand more. The fun she had with rhymes made learning feel like a game, and it made a real difference in her learning journey.

By leveraging neuroplasticity principles, you can tailor interventions to promote neural stimulation and enrich educational experiences. By building on learners' strengths and creating environments where fun and play are built into the foundation, learners can naturally experience trial and error. Therefore, they embrace failure as a natural part of the learning process. However, self-efficacy and agency are vital for the learner to go from the 'error' stage back to a new 'trial'. You can begin to stretch learners and design more challenging tasks, encouraging them to take risks and explore innovative solutions. Providing constructive feedback and celebrating effort, progress and resilience further reinforce a culture of continuous improvement.

Reflection ⑦

» Reflect on your own childhood experiences with rhymes and songs, and how they may have influenced your language development.

» Consider how you incorporate opportunities for multisensory approaches with your struggling learners to support their literacy development.

Clarity on personal identity

At the beginning of this chapter, I discussed the importance of enhancing the learning capacity of all. A fundamental aspect of this is the importance of empowering your learners to be communicators of their own thoughts. Educators play a crucial role in nurturing learners' communication skills and fostering self-expression. Encouraging students to articulate their thoughts, feelings and ideas through verbal and written communication promotes self-awareness and self-confidence (see Chapter 3). Providing opportunities for meaningful dialogue, reflection and expression enables students to develop their voices and advocate for themselves.

Creating a strengths-based approach in the classroom involves recognising and celebrating each learner's unique talents, interests and contributions. You can design inclusive learning experiences that showcase diverse abilities and perspectives, fostering a sense of belonging and appreciation for individual differences. I have found that creating an environment where choice and pupil voice are at the heart is one of the most effective ways of empowering and celebrating each learner's strengths and interests. Incorporating activities that promote active listening, empathy and perspective taking helps students understand the importance of effective communication in building relationships and navigating diverse social contexts. It is important to plan into class routines and timetables opportunities for students to share their talents, interests and achievements with their peers and the wider community.

Application

» **Create opportunities that ask learners to share their choices and preferences:** Ask about their favourite books and topics of interest, and for feedback on activities in terms of whether they enjoyed them, could they be improved and what helps them to learn best.

» **Place an emphasis on metacognition:** This involves modelling and demonstrating how we learn, as well as modelling the mistakes that we might make, the importance of repeating information to ourselves, or using graphic organisers to organise and remember key bits of information.

» **Provide opportunities for pupil voice feedback:** Ask learners what made a difference or helped them to learn specific things. If you are using coloured paper to make information more accessible to learners, ask them which colour makes a difference.

» **Create opportunities for choice:** Present a menu of options around where they work, what writing materials they use, how they present their work, and more.

» **Assign classroom jobs:** From sharpening pencils to organising resources, classroom jobs provide opportunities for learners to demonstrate strengths and develop responsibility and a sense of ownership.

Remember, creating a culture of ownership involves valuing learners' voices, embracing growth and allowing flexibility in how learning is demonstrated. When learners feel ownership, they become active participants in their own education.

Exploring Universal Design for Learning

In my work I advocate for a curriculum framework based around the principles of Universal Design for Learning (UDL). UDL emphasises proactive and flexible approaches to curriculum design, instruction and assessment that accommodate the diverse needs and preferences of all learners (CAST, 2018). By employing UDL principles, educators design instruction, materials and assessments that are accessible and engaging for every learner, regardless of their abilities or differences. This shift in focus to embracing how we can make learning inclusive for all reduces barriers and opens our minds to building learning capacity from the start. This places the emphasis back on us as educators, as people who need to be more analytical and forensic in our thinking.

Below is a case study that demonstrates how you can apply the three principles of UDL in the classroom.

CASE STUDY 🔊

Tom is a nine-year-old pupil diagnosed with dyslexia. Tom had been observed to particularly struggle with reading comprehension and written expression due to difficulties with processing and recalling information. To support Tom's learning, his teacher implemented a variety of UDL strategies tailored to his needs and strengths.

1.   **Providing multiple means of representation:** Using multiple formats (text, audio, video, visual aids such as graphic organisers) to help Tom better understand and organise information.

2.   **Multiple means of engagement:** Using alternative access to texts, using graphic novels, text to speech and digital books to support repetition, independent access, choice and enjoyment of print.

3.   **Multiple means of expression:** Using speech-to-text technology to allow Tom to verbally express his ideas and thoughts. Therefore, he is able to demonstrate his knowledge and edit and redraft his work, enabling him to have ownership of the creative process.

By offering flexible options for how information is presented and how Tom can respond, the teacher ensured that Tom can fully engage with the curriculum and demonstrate his knowledge effectively. Through these UDL strategies, Tom experienced increased access to learning and greater success in his educational journey.

Through the application of UDL, educators create an inclusive and supportive learning environment where all students can thrive and reach their full potential, promoting a label-free classroom where every learner is valued and empowered.

Summary

Beginning with their vision, values and expectations, educators play a pivotal role in initiating change within the learning environment. By recognising that the change starts with educators, not learners, the emphasis is on adjusting the learning environment to meet diverse needs. Rather than focusing on the differences, it is about finding the common ground and establishing high aspirations for all learners, highlighting the significance of creating an inclusive environment where each learner feels valued and supported.

Key takeaways 📝

»   Reflect on how your unique values, beliefs and experiences shape the identity of your learners.

»   Consider your class/school setting: are there opportunities for your learners to reflect on their and others' thoughts and feelings?

Further reading

- Made by Dyslexia (nd) [online] Available at: www.madebydyslexia.org (accessed 22 July 2024).
- Morgan, F C (2023) *Square Pegs: Inclusivity, Compassion and Fitting in – A Guide for Schools* (I Gilbert, ed). Carmarthen: Independent Thinking Press.
- Murphy, K (2023) *A Guide to Neurodiversity in the Early Years*. Anna Freud Centre. [online] Available at: www.annafreud.org/resources/under-fives-wellbeing/a-guide-to-neurodiversity-in-the-early-years/ (accessed 23 September 2024).
- Nutbrown, C (2011) *The Threads of Thinking*. London: Sage Publications.
- Quigley, A (2020) *Closing the Reading Gap*. Abingdon: Routledge.

References

Athey, C (2007) *Extending Thought in Young Children: A Parent–Teacher Partnership.* London: Paul Chapman Publishing.

Aubrey-Smith, F T (2023) Being Clear About Pedagogy. [online] Available at: https://edexec.co.uk/being-clear-about-pedagogy/ (accessed 23 September 2024).

CAST (2018) Universal Design for Learning Guidelines version 2.2. [online] Available at: http://udlguidelines.cast.org (accessed 22 July 2024).

Dix, P (2017) *When the Adults Change, Everything Changes: Seismic Shifts in School Behaviour.* Carmarthen: Independent Thinking Press.

Ehri, L C, Nunes, S R, Willows, D M, Schuster, B V, Yaghoub-Zadeh, Z and Shanahan, T (2001) Phonemic Awareness Instruction Helps Children Learn to Read: Evidence from the National Reading Panel's Meta-Analysis. *Reading Research Quarterly*, 36(3): 250–87.

Gathercole, S P (2008) *Working Memory and Learning: A Practical Guide for Teachers.* London: Sage Publications.

Heiskanen, N A (2018) Positioning Children with Special Educational Needs in Early Childhood Education and Care Documents. *British Journal of Sociology of Education*, 39(6): 827–43.

Moseley, S (2023) *Teaching Reading to All Learners Including Those with Complex Needs: A Framework for Progression within an Inclusive Reading Curriculum*. Abingdon: Routledge.

Swann, M P A (2012) *Creating Learning without Limits*. Maidenhead: Open University Press.

The Star Thrower (nd) Wikipedia: The Free Encyclopedia. [online] Available at: http://en.wikipedia.org/wiki/The_Star_Thrower (accessed 22 July 2024).

Vygotsky, L (2004) Imagination & Creativity in Childhood. *Journal of Russian & East European Psychology*, 42(1): 4–84.

Wolf, M (2008) *Proust and the Squid: The Story and Science of the Reading Brain*. New York: Harper Perennial.

5 Disability or determination?

AMANDA KIRBY

Introduction

How you view your students shapes the way you consider their potential. If you start with a view of what someone can't do rather than seeing the potential capacity, strengths and determination of that individual, you can limit their outcomes now and in the future.

Terms such as disability, and even the term 'special' if not fully understood, can result in limitations. Let me start by bringing clarity to the following key terms.

Disability

The term 'disability' pertains to a condition or conditions that may require specific accommodations or adjustments. An estimated 1.3 billion people – about 16 per cent of the global population – currently experience significant disability.

The World Health Organization (WHO) describes disability as follows: '*Disability is part of being human. Almost everyone will temporarily or permanently experience disability at some point in their life*' (WHO, nd). WHO further states that:

> *Disability results from the interaction between individuals with a health condition, such as Cerebral Palsy, Down syndrome and depression, with personal and environmental factors including negative attitudes, inaccessible transportation and public buildings, and limited social support.*
>
> (WHO, nd)

This perspective emphasises the environmental aspect of being disabled:

> *A person's environment has a huge effect on the experience and extent of disability. Inaccessible environments create barriers that often hinder the full and effective participation of persons with disabilities in society on an equal basis with others.*
>
> (WHO, nd)

The emphasis is also on finding ways to increase social participation when barriers are recognised and addressed.

Determination

The term 'determination' is a personal quality that can positively influence a student's approach to learning. It's essential for educators to recognise and support all students with disabilities while also fostering a positive and determined mindset to enhance overall academic success.

People of determination (POD)

People of determination is a term that has been used, for example, in Abu Dhabi. In this context it is being used to describe people who need assistance because of a disability that limits their intellectual and/or physical abilities.

Chapter aims

The core aim of this chapter is to describe the different aspects required to encourage the equitable participation, engagement and growth of all young people in education who experience barriers to engagement. The focus of this chapter is on what makes a young person thrive and succeed in education and life when they may be considered to be disabled or their environment disables them.

Barriers to success may be the environment a person is placed in, the attitudes of others and the tasks they are being asked to do which could be adapted or avoided.

Figure 5.1 *Three core barriers to success addressed in this chapter*

In this chapter, I seek to cover seven key questions.

1. What *attitudes* of the educator, the parent, peers and the student best facilitate inclusion and engagement?

2. What levels of *awareness* by the educator, the parent, peers and the student are required?

3. How can you *gain knowledge* through observation, assessment and gathering information from different informants while recognising the developmental milestones?

4. How to support the individual to be their best self?

5. Why does seeking strengths through failure matter and how?

6. How can you make sense of and understand changing brains?

7. How can you plan for the future and times of change?

Attitudes

This pertains to the educator, the parent and the student.

Educator

The attitude of the people around the student both at home and at school can make a real difference to engagement and participation. As an educator, you can lack information about the student that can result in different assumptions about the student's potential, or you can be presented with reports from others that can then result in you seeing a student in a certain way. Old assessment reports may represent a student that was very different four or five years ago and who is now able to undertake many of the tasks that they were incapable of doing at that time.

CASE STUDY ⊕

A less experienced teacher may be presented with a student in their class with physical challenges. This may be the first time that they have encountered a learner with these specific challenges. This may make them feel nervous about how to interact appropriately and safely and be unsure what to expect of the student. They may not allow the student to fully engage in some activities because of a fear of harm. The teacher may assume, for example, that a student with cerebral palsy may be unable to join in with certain tasks or sporting activities.

In such a scenario, mentoring from an experienced member of staff is advised.

You can also come with a set of biases based on other students you have taught in the past or from personal experiences you have had in your own life. These can shape your attitudes and actions. We need to be reminded that a student is far more than a diagnosis or label.

Parents

Parental approaches to schools will vary enormously and may be based on their current and past experiences in the school or in other schools. A parent can feel anxious about what someone thinks or says about their child, and it can make them more defensive. Some parents will have gained an extensive understanding not only of their child but of the condition or conditions their child is living with. They may come to school thinking they need to fight for their child, and this can sometimes feel like a win/lose situation rather than being on the same side working out together how to best allow the student to thrive, develop and grow.

Application 🔳

» Stress the importance of common goals of student progress in all your communications.

Some parents may also have had similar challenges in their lives if they have barriers to living and learning. Many neurodivergent children, for example, may have undiagnosed neurodivergent parents too. Considering that this may be why a parent may be defensive is important, as they may be reliving their past negative experiences and are concerned these may be repeated for their child (see Chapter 1).

The student

The student's attitude and self-concept will often be framed by the words and attitudes of those around them. They may not recognise the potential they have. Their attitude not to try something new may be because of fear of failing in front of peers and result in them not even believing new skills are possible for them. Parents and teachers may have set up situations that meant the student has not been allowed to take any risks at all. By understanding that learning also means failing and celebrating the steps taken in trying, you can help the learner see that failing is a part of learning. This is something that may need to be explicitly discussed with the student.

Awareness is key

No teacher can be knowledgeable about every medical condition, nor should they be. Most teachers need to have some knowledge about common cognitive traits, for example, as challenges with these can impact learning and participation. These could relate to skills such as learning to read, spell, write, communicate, socialise, learn mathematical operations and participate in age-appropriate sporting activities.

The good thing is that if you are working in a class of 20–30 students of a similar age from a similar background, you can see what skills most of those children can achieve when taught appropriately and practised sufficiently. If you are teaching a new age group, you may have less experience of what 'typical' can look like and when there are 'red flags'.

Make time to look at the table in the Appendix (p 93), which focuses mostly on typical developmental milestones of primary school children. This age band is focused on because it exhibits the greatest developmental variation. If 'red flags' are noted, you may want to consider gaining additional information or specialist support to explore this more, especially if the students are in an older age band.

Knowledge about different disabilities can be gained from different sources. This is especially true if a student has a condition which is less commonly seen such as a rare genetic condition. Knowledge may be gained during teacher training or later through postgraduate courses. Information can also be learned from other colleagues with greater experience around you. In some cases, you may need specific specialist training to gain confidence in supporting a student with a specific set of disabilities. Tapping into information from voluntary sector organisations nationally and locally can be a great help. Local health professional services can be a source of advice too.

Parental knowledge about their child's condition can vary hugely. Many parents can feel very alone, and it may have taken time for a diagnosis to be gained or they may still be exploring what are the reasons for their child's challenges. They may not know where to go to for advice and come to the educator to ask them what to do and what assistance is available to them. Signposting them to groups and voluntary sector organisations with support networks can be a game changer for many parents. In different countries there will be different pathways to support and intervention, and some of these will also have legal frameworks to comply with. This may mean there are timelines for specific actions too. Within a school setting you may be able to help create parental support networks where parents can share experiences and be able to support each other. Even providing a room to meet once a month for the meetings to take place can have a huge impact for many families.

Peer awareness

Most importantly, the student may also feel isolated from their peers. They may have a disability that makes them consider themselves to be different from their peers and they can feel a sense of shame or difference. Online groups and local support groups where they can meet other students who have similar experiences can be important, especially if young people are trying to form a sense of their selves. This is particularly true in the teen years where having peers can be so important. This may be achieved through virtual networks such as Facebook groups as well as local face-to-face groups. Many of these are run by local or national charities who support specific conditions.

One group that is not always considered is the peers' knowledge in school about another student's disability. Even more important is understanding the student's ability so they can engage with others in their educational life. Discussing with students what each person has in common is as important as discussing and respecting our differences. These are important lessons that can benefit everyone. Discussions about how our brains develop and change throughout our lives are important for every student.

Gaining knowledge

To design individual educational plans, we need to build a complete picture of that student. This allows us to understand the pace of learning and, the developmental phase the student is at and to grade activities in a way that works for them. We all learn differently and may need to do a task in a different way to reach the end point. Some students will need to use technology to express themselves, for example. A child with developmental co-ordination disorder may find handwriting hard to do and the use of speech-to-text software or teaching them to type can be a game changer to see them express their ideas and knowledge with others.

Often we can make assumptions that are gathered from our own experiences, and these can be limiting. We may see a student only at home or only at school and not see other parts of that student that are very different. A student with their pet dog may change the way they express themselves; another student who plays with their siblings at home may be caring and funny in a safe environment. Finding out information from multiple sources about a student, including listening to the 'voice' of the child, is so important.

Gaining knowledge about a student can come through different routes and over time. This can be through observation, standardised assessments and finding out information from different informants. Parents need to see they are valued, and their input is appreciated, listened to and valued. If we only ask but don't do anything with this information, they may instantly feel devalued.

Listening to the voice of the child is essential to ensure this is considered in all planning. What motivates, interests or inspires a child can be a way to open the door to engagement. Children don't always have a voice, and they may communicate what they want and think also through their feelings. The support of a key person who gets to know the child can enable them to begin to make sense of and understand the world, manage their feelings, and feel safe and confident in expressing their views. The child also needs to see their input is valued. This needs to be done at all review stages too.

When designing individual educational plans, we need to synthesise all the information gathered from multiple sources to help inform the design of the plans and ensure the plan reflects the 'whole student'.

Supporting the individual to be their best self

In the context of education, it's increasingly recognised that disability is not solely an individual trait but that an inability to participate and engage may be shaped by the interplay between that person and their environment. Researchers in the field of rehabilitation science emphasise the crucial role of environmental factors in influencing the health and well-being of individuals. The World Health Organization's International Classification of Functioning, Disability, and Health (ICF 20) underscores this perspective, proposing that disability emerges from the interaction between impairments and the environment. However, it doesn't delve into the specific mechanisms through which individuals and their surroundings interact.

While the social model of disability explains how societal organisation can impact individuals and contribute to disability, it falls short in illustrating how individuals, in turn, influence their social environments and the reciprocal nature of this interaction. It's crucial to distinguish between interaction and transaction in this context. Interaction signifies a mutual or reciprocal action, while transaction implies that one element alters the usual activity of another, either quantitatively or qualitatively. This can be a positive discussion in education about what the student with a disability can offer to others around them and what they can learn too.

Understanding these dynamics is essential in fostering an inclusive educational environment where the reciprocal relationship between individuals and their surroundings is considered. Setting up the environment for success can make a real difference. If we can understand that some students, for example, can find certain sensory settings uncomfortable, making it hard for them to learn, we can see that when we create an environment that optimises their learning this has the opposite effect. For example, some students may get upset by loud noises and chatter in the playground: by wearing headphones to reduce the sounds, they can happily engage. Another child may have difficulties with responding verbally but by using text-to-speech technology they can become part of a team and actively contribute.

'*Tell me and I forget, teach me and I may remember, involve me and I learn*', said Benjamin Franklin. We need to check that the way we are delivering information is accessible for all students to ensure participation, understanding and active engagement. Asking the student what they think can be humbling but it ensures we stay sharp about what inclusion is all about. Considering what may need to be avoided, adapted and adjusted to ensure this happens is always important.

Seeking strengths through failing

> ### Reflection ⑦
>
> » How do we know what a student's strengths are?

Finding what excites, motivates and provides pleasure for one student can differ so much compared to another. If we can engage a student fully, it can lead to new discoveries and improved outcomes. When a student is engaged, we can see the real determination in what they want to achieve.

This often means a student may need to be exposed to a variety of opportunities to see what is possible. If you only allow a child to stay in their (or your) comfort zone, they can never experience what they could do and realise their full potential.

Trying out new experiences may feel risky. It is a fine balance between taking risks that could result in harm (which we want to always avoid) and not allowing a student to take any risks at all. In some cases, we can be overprotective. It can mean that a student also has no experience of failure. We may also need to discuss how we all fail at times, and it is an important part of learning. Think about many toddlers learning to walk; how many times do they fall over before they start to move independently?

Goal setting at an appropriate level with each student is important. We need to make these steps small and potentially achievable, so if they are not achieved the student (with the parent and/or teacher) can learn from them and we can try to reset the goals.

Researchers in Canada developed a process used in the field of developmental co-ordination disorder called CO-OP (Schwartz et al, 2020). This process involves a cycle of actions described as '*Goal, Plan, Do and Review*': set the goals; create an understandable and accessible plan; do the actions; and review what worked or not and then set a new set of goals. This cycle can be applied to all aspects of learning.

By celebrating the efforts taken and the learning gained, even if this is in very small steps, we can begin to see failure as a positive way of building resilience. However, we may also need to discuss that learning new skills can also mean we need to tolerate some discomfort. There may be a need to practise a skill sufficiently and in appropriate settings before we can feel confident the skill has been attained. If we, as educators, can also share what we have learned from our failures we could also help others with their learning too.

Preparing for times of change

Our brains continue to change throughout our lives. There are two major growth and development phases in children's brains.

The brain in the first couple of years of life is highly plastic, meaning it is adaptable and responsive to experiences. Varied and enriching learning experiences during early years can positively shape neural connections. Teachers need to provide a diverse range of stimulating activities to foster optimal brain development. Neuroplasticity persists throughout our lives but at a slower rate compared to early childhood. This means there is always the potential for change and for learning to take place. Lifelong learning is key to consider. Fostering a growth mindset in students, emphasising that the brain can continue to adapt and grow through effort and perseverance, is an important message to give to students. This means they can see change and growth is possible at every stage of life.

Emerging adulthood is the second critical time for massive changes in our brains. This is the name given to the important phase bridging adolescence and adulthood, where the individual is usually still dependent on their parents. This stage is more common in industrialised countries, where economically, and so practically, adolescents may have time for social and workplace experimentation before settling into adulthood. Emerging adulthood has also been described as a distinct period in terms of identity exploration where the individual can develop their own ideas and views independent to those of their parents. Emerging adults must also develop greater consideration for others, learn social norms and comply with them, and create a value system for themselves in the context of their society. This is usually described as the years between 11 and 25 years. Developing good self-worth and perception is important for all teenagers, where peer-to-peer acceptance becomes more important than adult–peer relationships. This means acknowledging and respecting individual identities in the classroom. Educators need to provide opportunities for self-expression and exploration to support all students in developing a strong sense of self. There is a need to provide a safe and supportive environment that helps students develop their emotional skills.

The brain goes through a process of synaptic pruning during emerging adulthood where unnecessary neural connections are eliminated, making the brain more efficient. One part of the brain that particularly goes through major changes during emerging adulthood is the pre-frontal cortex, which is responsible for emotional regulation. This means at this time children can be more disinhibited and take more risks. Supporting emotional regulation in the classroom at all phases of development is important.

Application ⌗

» The relevance for teaching means focusing and building the essential skills for independent life and at the same time being aware of not cognitively overloading the student.

» Providing frameworks to help develop executive functioning skills can be helpful at every stage of development but especially in this phase.

» Encouraging critical thinking and problem-solving skills is also essential. Skills need to be presented at a level that the student can take on board. Simple tools like colour coding, labelling, teaching sorting, use of writing frames, diaries and time management tools can have a lasting impact for all students and can be introduced at all stages of education.

Understanding these brain changes can guide teachers in creating developmentally appropriate learning experiences. Tailoring teaching strategies to align with the evolving cognitive and emotional needs of students enhances the effectiveness of classroom practices.

Planning for the future

When planning for times of transition for students with disabilities, there are several considerations that you should keep in mind. It's crucial to create an inclusive and supportive environment that addresses the specific needs of each student. Learners might be transitioning into new environments, out of familiar environments or up into the next stages of education or employment. Here are ten key considerations for different transition periods.

1. **Individualised transition plans (ITPs):** Develop individualised plans for each disabled student, taking into account their unique abilities, challenges and goals. Collaborate with parents, special education professionals and other relevant stakeholders to create comprehensive ITPs.

2. **Early planning and communication:** Start the transition planning process early to ensure a smooth transition. Communicate with both the students and their parents or guardians about upcoming changes and involve everyone in the decision-making processes.

3. **Accessibility of physical spaces:** Ensure that physical spaces, including classrooms, hallways and common areas, are accessible for students who have access challenges. This may involve making adjustments such as ramps, lifts and accessible toilets.

4. **Curriculum and instructional adaptations:** Modify the curriculum and instructional methods to accommodate the diverse needs of the student. Don't assume needs or adaptations by diagnosis. Provide appropriate resources, tools and technologies to support their learning.

5. **Staff training:** Conduct training sessions for school staff to raise awareness and build expertise on working with specific students. This includes understanding different disabilities, implementing assistive technologies, and fostering a supportive and inclusive classroom culture.

6. **Emotional and social support:** Recognise and address the emotional and social aspects of transitions. Foster a positive and inclusive school culture where students feel supported and accepted by their peers. Allow the student time to get used to the new environment, which may in reality take a term or two.

7. **Transition to post-school life:** For older students, consider their transition to post-school life, including higher education, vocational training or employment. Collaborate with relevant agencies and organisations to facilitate a seamless transition. The conversation about post-school transition should start as soon as possible.

8. **Communication tools:** Implement effective communication tools, such as visual schedules, social stories or assistive communication devices, to aid understanding and participation for students with communication challenges.

9. **Regular assessment and adjustment:** Continuously assess the effectiveness of any transition plan and make adjustments as needed. Regularly communicate with parents and other stakeholders to gather feedback and insights. This may take several iterations to get it right and it will need to be reviewed regularly.

10. **Legal compliance:** Ensure compliance with legal requirements, such as the Equality Act 2010, which prohibits discrimination against individuals with disabilities. Familiarise yourself with relevant policies and procedures to protect the rights of disabled students.

By addressing these considerations, teachers can contribute to creating an inclusive and supportive educational environment for disabled students during times of transition and ensure they can showcase their talents and skills.

Key takeaways 📝

» What, by your definition, is a disability?

» How do we identify strengths and build resilience in all students?

» How do we view failure and risk-taking?

» Does everyone need to play team games to become an active and engaged adult?

» Does everyone need to write neatly when we have technology that can provide alternative means of communication?

Editors' note

Re-read the chapter and make some notes on how you would relate this to agency, breakthrough and identity, the core threads of this book.

Further reading

- **Appendix:** Developmental norms, 4–11 years (page 93).

- Dibden, E (2019) 'People of Determination': A Better Term for SEND? *TES*, 4 January. [online] Available at: www.tes.com/magazine/archive/people-determination-better-term-send (accessed 22 July 2024).

- Kirby, A and Smith, T (2021) *Neurodiversity at Work: Drive Innovation, Performance and Productivity with a Neurodiverse Workforce*. London and New York: Kogan Page.

- Kirby, A, Ellis, P and Osbourne, A (2023) *Neurodiversity and Education*. London: Corwin Publishers.

- Lele, P (2023) People of Determination—Making Achievements, Overcoming Challenges. In Uniyal, R and Rizvi, F (eds) *Understanding Disability* (pp 181–94). Singapore: Springer.

- Leonardi M et al (2022) 20 Years of ICF-International Classification of Functioning, Disability and Health: Uses and Applications Around the World. *International Journal of Environmental Research and Public Health*, 19(18): 11321.

- UAE Government (2024) People of Determination. [online] Available at: https://u.ae/en/information-and-services/social-affairs/people-of-determination (accessed 22 July 2024).

References

Schwartz, S P, Northrup, S R K, Izadi-Najafabadi, S and Zwicker, J G (2020) CO-OP for Children with DCD: Goals Addressed and Strategies Used. *Canadian Journal of Occupational Therapy*, 87(4): 278–86.

World Health Organization (WHO) (nd) Disability. [online] Available at: www.who.int/health-topics/disability (accessed 22 July 2024).

6 Helplessness or hope?

SUE JAGGER

Introduction

Hope is defined by the Concise Oxford English Dictionary as *'a feeling of expectation and desire'*. This concept was central to my choice to train to be a teacher over 25 years ago, the belief in becoming a teacher who can make a difference to the lives of the students I teach. Hope remains central to my pedagogical practice today, the belief that I can enable others to thrive and believe that the next day can be better. Every time I plan a lesson, I hope that it will make a difference to students, increasing their curiosity to explore the concepts, knowledge and skills, ensuring that together we learn. Hope is also central to my role as a parent. Parents everywhere value the belief that their child will thrive and achieve the very best that they can.

In contrast helplessness is defined (by the Concise Oxford English Dictionary) as *'uncontrollable'*, *'unable to defend oneself, to act without help'*. And yes, there have been times in my roles as both a parent and a classroom teacher that I have experienced a sense of helplessness. A sense that I failed. A sense that I have not achieved my full potential and therefore not enabled those around me, my children or my students, to achieve to the best of their ability, to be the best they could be. A sense that my belief, my expectation, was misplaced, a sense of helplessness, a lack of control resulting in vulnerability. However, I have learnt that hope can be far more powerful than any other emotion in terms of learning and being a parent. It encourages motivation and creates resilience and a sense of achievement.

Our daughter was diagnosed as 'autistic with a PDA (pathological demand avoidance) profile' at the age of 16. I have throughout my career taught many neurodiverse students and learnt a great deal from them. The one thing that I feel I have learnt from both our daughter and my students is that the labels ascribed to them do not define who they are or what they can achieve. It is this positive approach to labels that I would like to explore in this chapter – my belief, my hope that a label helps us to understand, not to define or to limit expectations.

Chapter aims ◎

This chapter addresses seven questions, around three core themes.

Active agency

1.   Does a diagnosis define a learner?

2.   How often as a classroom teacher do you listen to your students explaining themselves as learners?

Breakthrough

3.   The learner's voice is both powerful and desirable. How effectively do you use this to go beyond 'consistently inconsistent' and 'predictably unpredictable' labels to understand the learner's own self-awareness and self-perception?

4.   Is the teacher–student relationship the most important teaching and learning tool in the classroom? Should this come before a label of diagnosis?

Clarity

5.   Language is the key to understanding; how often as a teacher do you consciously consider your language choices?

6.   Hope that a student can access and learn requires a classroom culture that enables students to achieve. How as a teacher can you craft a classroom culture for each of your students?

And finally

7.   How often in your classroom do you consider the difference and gap between the teacher saying '*This is who you are*' and learners confidently stating '*This is who I am*'.

Reflection ⑦

»   Take some time to consider the questions above.

»   Write down the key connotations for you in your classroom.

There is nothing more effective than listening to your child; they are often more perceptive than we are as adults. My daughter and I were recently talking about what autism meant to her and I believe that her response was quite insightful.

Well, I know what autism isn't, it isn't that I don't like fireworks. (Daughter)

What do you mean? (Sue)

Well, I was talking to someone the other day about fireworks, and I said that I don't like them. (Daughter)

They said, "That's because you're autistic." (Daughter)

It's really annoying. Why can't it just be because I don't like fireworks? Why does someone have to say it's because I am autistic? Being autistic just means that I see the world differently and sometimes I don't understand why someone thinks I might have been rude; it doesn't mean I have to like fireworks. (Daughter)

Our daughter was able to clearly articulate her feelings about being labelled as 'autistic'. Her comments led me to reflect upon my practice as a teacher – how often had I been presented with the diagnosis of a student before meeting them, particularly at the beginning of a new academic year, and then through these details begun to form a model in my mind about how this learner might act, react or even interact within my classroom environment? It was a stark suggestion and led me to ask myself the question, '*Do I provide the students in my class with a voice and opportunity to say who they are as learners?*'

CASE STUDY ⏣

Does a diagnosis define a student?

Class teachers across the globe engage with new classes at some point in the year, most often in September. Often the reflections of teachers within a workroom are '*I wonder what my new class will be like?*' I have heard teachers on many occasions discuss with one another the profile of former groups: '*You used to teach this group – what are they like? What needs do they have?*' Class data in the form of attainment grades, diagnosis and progression trajectories are shared, along with other written records. But to what ends? Are these shared comments useful? Or is it more useful for a teacher to wait until they meet a class before they learn the labels? Maybe over the holidays, a growth or maturation process has taken place and students are returning different to when they left the previous year. I teach in a mainstream secondary school that has several support units for special educational needs and disabilities (SEND): one for students with communication challenges, one for students with hearing impairment and another for visually impaired students. A recent class that I was going to teach had ten children within the class (of 28) who between them had 34 diagnosed conditions. I felt that the diagnosis of the students would not enable me to build what I see as the most crucial teaching strategy: the teacher–student relationship. It is often the practice in schools for teachers to prepare seating plans before they meet a new class.

In recent years, I have stopped trying to write a seating plan for the students I have not yet met. This has enabled me to take my time to identify the needs of the students I am just getting to know and to begin to work with the students rather than to work with their diagnosis. Seating plans do have a place in the classroom; they are particularly useful if a member of staff is absent and a cover teacher is trying to use the correct names for each student. However, I feel that organising a seating plan based upon academic data and SEND

→

diagnosis is counterproductive, as it is based upon the label and not the individual. Our daughter's diagnosis has enabled her rather than disabled her. In fact, I would argue that prior to her diagnosis she was 'disabled' because she was frightened of her own emotional responses, unsure of why she reacted or overreacted to a scenario. Now, following her diagnosis, as you can see from her earlier comments about fireworks, she has begun to understand herself more and now has the agency to be able to express why she responds in an unpredictable manner at times. Her teachers are also aware of how to interact with and support her to enable her to be the best she can be.

I believe that the students in my class know themselves and should be given a chance to express themselves as learners within an effective classroom culture. I am currently trialling a seating plan that shows the student's name and strategies that I can use to engage the student, rather than labels for a diagnosis. This is part of my classroom culture because as we work together and the students talk more about what can support them, this working document changes and adapts to their needs.

Application

» Consider how you might plan a seating plan for one of your classes using their names and pedagogical strategies rather than names and labels. It might look like Figure 6.1.

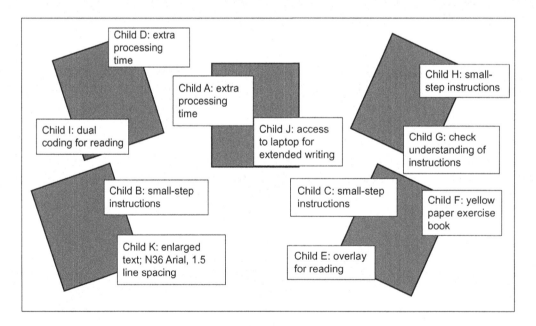

Figure 6.1 *Seating plan with supportive strategies for each student with a neurodiverse diagnosis*

Application 🗒️

Another way that a seating plan can be organised to support a teacher's recognition of students' required support can be seen in the following approach that Anita Devi developed (see Figure 6.2, which answers the overriding question: Where do I start?).

I have found that adopting this strategy-focused seating plan has provided me with a positive approach to my teaching. It means that when I walk in the classroom, I know that the students are able to achieve and understand that their diagnosis does not define them; it supports them.

	Class Layout	Resources	Learning	Rewards	
Child 1	Not next to AB				
Child 2	L-handed	Concrete	2 chunks at a time		
Child 3		Concrete			
Child 4	Near front	Void blank sheet Use AMR	Ask to repeat instructions		
Child 5			Ask to repeat instructions	Doesn't value HPs	
Child 6	Away from noise	Visual	Small groups		
Child 7					
Child 8	Clear sight of board	Concrete			

Figure 6.2 *Multiple needs in the classroom – adaptations from a place of strength – what works!* (Devi, 2023)

Reflection ❓

» How do you ensure that the diagnosis of your students supports their learning?

» As a class teacher, do you allow yourself time to get to know your students?

» How do you ensure that you listen to the students as they reveal how they learn more effectively?

CASE STUDY 🄬

How can we create a classroom culture for each of our students?

The Concise Oxford English Dictionary defines learning as '*knowledge or skills acquired through experience or study or by being taught*'. It states that 'teach' finds its origins in the Old English *tæcan*, '*show, present, point out*'; this is exactly what I do as a classroom teacher. I feel that as a teacher I am a facilitator; I show students the exciting aspects of learning and create a classroom environment that enables them to learn. I support students to understand themselves as learners and to engage with the subject they are studying.

I currently teach English, both English language and English literature. English is a complex subject to study and involves a learner understanding their own thoughts, beliefs and perceptions, and learning how to apply them to the texts we are exploring. English, as with other subject disciplines, demands the modalities of talk, reading and writing to ensure that a learner can communicate clearly and with coherence about the concepts they are exploring. When learning occurs it is often an emotive process, and one that can make the learner vulnerable. The very fact that the learner is learning suggests that there is something that is new to them or a concept that they may have to unlearn or relearn. With this 'newness' comes a sense of vulnerability. Being vulnerable for any of us can be challenging; being neurodiverse in a mainstream classroom and being exposed to concepts of a subject discipline can be incredibly challenging. Vulnerability can cause the sense of a lack of control, a sense of helplessness. The environment in which the learning is taking place is of critical importance. A teacher knowing and understanding their students is central to the success of a learning culture within a classroom.

As a classroom teacher, I need to work with my students to ensure that the range of emotions from vulnerable to confident is recognised, valued and owned to ensure that learning can be a productive experience for all. As a classroom teacher, I am responsible for the learning culture in my classroom.

The learning culture in a classroom is the responsibility of the class teacher, who provides students with a safe space in which they can take risks, make mistakes or have misconceptions that empower them to move forward in their understanding. A teacher needs to be conscious of their own crucial role in the creation of their classroom culture. While I believe all the elements combine to create a classroom culture, the language we use is imperative to a student's engagement, learning and progress. The language a teacher uses, how they value talk and how the teacher frames the student's learning experience and presents concepts are key to their learning experience. I have learnt as both a practitioner and a parent that the language we use to communicate with a neurodiverse student is key to being able to build a relationship with them and to understanding their barriers to learning.

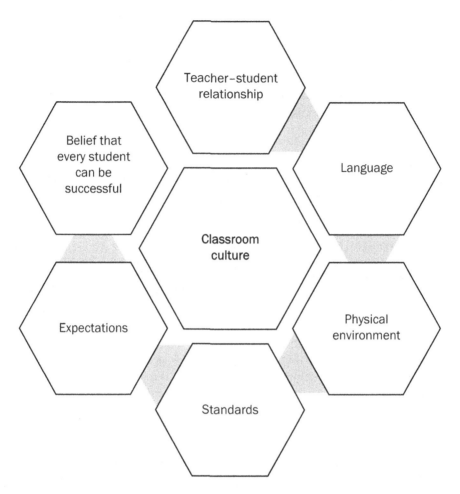

Figure 6.3 *Elements that contribute to create a classroom culture*

Application 🔲

Declaratives not imperatives

» Consider how you use language in your classroom to craft a culture of learning.

Our choice of language as a classroom teacher is vital. It sets the tone of the lesson and learning over time. For example, if I choose to use imperatives within my classroom such as '*Shut the door*', I am making my expectations clear and directing the students to follow my instructions. However, this directive that can seem very simple to most of us can trigger anxiety and an impulse response, such as shouting, refusal to follow an instruction or rudeness in a neurodiverse student. Many neurodiverse students are impulsive in their responses and will often mirror the way they perceive they are being spoken to. If a student perceives a teacher as raising their voice, then they will often raise their voice in response. It is not unusual for a neurodiverse student to be perceived as rude, when in fact they are copying the communication choices of the initiator of the dialogue. It is therefore important for us as teachers to have an awareness of the tone we choose.

The vocabulary we choose is equally important. A neurodiverse student often has single-dimension thinking and therefore has a very definite understanding that they will apply to the language being used. For example, I can remember in my very early days of teaching suggesting to a small group of students that they needed '*to pull their socks up*', at which point the neurodiverse student in the group immediately bent down and pulled up his socks! This was the result of my miscommunication and lack of recognition of the need for clarity in my vocabulary.

Many of us have carefully planned routines in our classrooms to ensure that students can enter the classroom and learning can begin quickly. It is important that we recognise how we verbally frame our expectations through our vocabulary. Our expectations might appear to be very simple, for example, in our school when students enter the classroom, they are expected to organise their equipment ready to learn. They must place their planner, their pencil case and their reading book on their desk. This is a clear expectation; however, some students do forget. When I remind them, I have to consider the vocabulary I use. I could say '*Get your planner out*', which appears to be a straightforward instruction. However, this can raise anxiety, particularly for a student with PDA (pathological demand avoidance); therefore, I would use a phrase such as '*It would be helpful if everyone had their planners out on their tables*'. Just by removing the imperative 'get', the level of anxiety has declined, resulting in increased compliance and allowing students to meet the expectation. The use of enabling and encouraging language crafts a positive learning environment. Consider the phrase '*Thank you for listening*' rather than '*Can you stop talking please*' or '*It would be helpful if someone could pass me that book*' rather than '*Give me that book*'. The use of declaratives rather than imperatives is much softer and less confrontational, but the expectation and outcome remain the same. There is hope in our classroom culture that can be seen through the vocabulary of our choice.

Reflection ⑦

» How do you create a culture within your own classroom?

» How often do you reflect upon your choice of language as a classroom teacher?

» How do you enable your students through your classroom culture?

Robin Alexander (2013, p 3) states that *'talk makes a unique and powerful contribution to children's development, thinking and learning'*. I believe that it is not only the student who benefits from talk within the classroom, but the teacher too. When a teacher talks with a student they learn a great deal, but when they listen to a student and hear that student's voice the teacher learns so much more. Sitting and talking to a student can be a challenge in a busy classroom, but it is essential if the teacher is to understand the student's needs.

CASE STUDY ⊕

The learner's voice is both powerful and desirable

How effectively do we use the learner's voice to go beyond 'consistently inconsistent' and 'predictably unpredictable' labels to understand the learner's own self-awareness and self-perception?

Students all have their own interests and preferred ways of receiving and processing information. Some students enjoy talking, some reading quietly; others just like to record their ideas, whether this is in the written form or in a drawing. As a class teacher it is important for me to know and understand the students' preferences. Understanding the students' preferences and what is most effective for them comes through observing and listening. This can be challenging. As a parent of a child who can be 'predictably unpredictable', having a bank of engagement strategies is key. For example, when asked to go and put something in the bin, our daughter will not be able to do this because she sees it as a demand and can become overwhelmed at the thought. However, if I say, '*I bet you can't put that in the bin in less than three minutes*', she will immediately light up and race towards the bin.

Finding out what works for each student takes time. Giving time to each student in a classroom can be a challenge; however, it is key to unlocking their ability to learn within the culture of your classroom. Talking to students and finding out who they are as a learner is important. When our daughter was diagnosed, a friend of mine who also has a neurodiverse child said, '*You will be fine so long as you realise that your life will now be predictably unpredictable and consistently inconsistent*' – it was the best piece of advice we had. It is so true; neurodiverse students are predictably unpredictable – one day they may be quite focused and the next they might not be able to sit down and focus. It is therefore important to have a series of approaches that you can use to engage students, and these come from taking time to build a positive student–teacher relationship and through talk. The repetition of the strategies over time helps to make the unpredictable more predictable, which is neuroplasticity.

Application 🔳

Talk is key to understanding

I have previously taught a neurodiverse student who found it challenging at times to be able to sit in their seat for a duration of more than a few moments. Obviously, this prevented them from completing their written tasks and was distracting to those around them. I needed to understand what the student knew about themselves as a learner, their preferences and their dislikes. I needed to identify a strategy that would enable them to sit down for increasing periods of time, a strategy that if it were repeated would develop the student's behaviour and support them to learn. I needed to understand the student as a learner to identify a suitable strategy. The student's initial comment as they entered the English classroom was '*I don't like English*' or '*I don't like reading*'. I needed to reassure this student, but at the same time encourage them to engage. I therefore responded with '*I hear what you are saying – shall we try this?*' – the 'this' would be a task to distract them from their initial anxiety. Through our discussions the student mentioned maths and shapes. I wondered if this could be a way forward. I decided to laminate a selection of different shapes in a range of colours. I would have these available at the beginning of each lesson and would ask the student to choose a colour that they would try today. I did this in a one-to-one conversation, so that no other student was aware of this agreement. I would then find the correct laminated card and place this on the chair that the student was to sit on. The shape would be upside down to encourage the student to take the responsibility to turn the shape over and check that it was the correct one. I would then say '*quick, before anyone sees it*' and the student would sit down on the shape. Over a prolonged time, two terms, the student was able to sit for longer and the shapes took a back step, but this was the first step to engagement with their learning. Key to this strategy working were several aspects:

» the recognition of the student's barrier to learning, without judgement;

» listening to the student talking about themselves and identifying what engaged them, recognising that they understand themselves as a learner – this student knew that they like maths and shapes;

» the hope and belief that over time the student's behaviour would alter due to repetition of a strategy; neuroplasticity supports the behaviours of the student in the classroom, enabling them to continue to learn.

Summary

In this chapter I have explained how the concept of 'hope' is essential to teaching and learning. Talking with and listening to our students is key to enable them, giving them the agency that they need to engage as learners.

Key takeaways 📖

» How often in our classrooms do we consider the difference and gap between teachers saying '*This is who you are*' and learners confidently stating '*This is who I am*'.

» Pause for a moment and consider the most recent lesson you taught. Did you enable your students to express themselves as learners? Did you enable them with the agency they need to confidently state who they are as learners?

Enabling a learner to discover their identity not only engenders curiosity, but also increases independence and interdependence with peers in the classroom.

Further reading

- Grandin, T and Panek, R (2014) *The Autistic Brain*. London: Rider, an imprint of Ebury Publishing.
- Grant, C and Grant, D (2023) *A Very Modern Family*. London: Piatkus.
- Morgan, N (2013) *Blame My Brain*. London: Walker Books.

References

Alexander, R J (2013) Improving Oracy and Classroom Talk: Achievements and Challenges. *Primary First*, 10: 22–9.

Devi, A (2023) *SEND Leadership Lens: Whole Setting Approach to Leading Adaptive Teaching*. TeamADL. [online] Available at: www.teamadl.uk (accessed 22 June 2024).

Stevenson, A and Waite, M (2011) *Concise Oxford English Dictionary*. Oxford: Oxford University Press.

7 Sensitivity or self-awareness?

ANITA DEVI

Introduction

All schools are required to promote the spiritual, moral, social and cultural (SMSC) development of learners. In England this is a statutory requirement. This imperatively imbibes a two-pronged approach – firstly, generic and ongoing education through the school ethos, norms and routines and, secondly, more specifically through direct instruction and teaching through personal, social, health and economic education (PSHE) curriculum, as well as through citizenship or relationships and sex education (RSE).

As a classroom practitioner, I've come across many children who present with a variety of needs, including cognition and learning and communication and interaction, yet at another level they connect with SMSC aspects of the curriculum or school life. For some the word connect would be a word of contention and they would seek to ask, '*How do I know and how do I measure connectedness?*' Interestingly, the Speech and Language UK Report in 2023 was entitled *Listening to Unheard Children*. SMSC by its very nature is language rich and yet we know that in 2023, Speech and Language UK reported 1.9 million children were struggling with talking and understanding words. So alongside this, are we failing them in SMSC education? How do we listen to unheard children? To understand this, deeper enquiry and understanding is required as to how learning in the classroom takes place.

As learners (either formally in education or lifelong through experiences), we receive information via our senses. Some cognitive neuroscientists would consider individual sensory receptors, stating we have around 33 mechanisms feeding our brain with information. Others in the field consider eight sensory systems, that is, the main five receptors: visual, auditory, olfactory, gustatory and tactile system plus two integration sensory systems (vestibular and proprioceptive) and finally sensations related to internal organs (interception). Previously, I have tended to focus on the first seven (Devi, 2020).

Each sensory system carries information to and from the brain. Some organs also have a dual purpose. For example, the tongue is involved in discerning taste, as well as aiding speech. This chapter focuses on the interplay between cognitive learning and communication systems. More specifically, I invite you to look beyond what is expected to what could be adapted. In the main, we communicate through non-verbal signals (that others receive), speech (that others interpret) and the written word (information that others read). I do not claim to have all the answers, as many cases are complex and unique to the individual. However, it is my intent that the chapter provokes further thought and inquiry.

Chapter aims ◎

This chapter addresses seven questions, around three core themes.

Activate agency

1. How do we ignite and record communicative learning in those who have no verbalised speech and/or cannot write through traditional methods?

2. How do we provide choice for those who cannot speak?

Breakthrough

3. Can the speech part of our brain be rewired?

4. What does breakthrough in learning or memory look like?

Clarity on personal identity

5. How does SMSC education further personal identity?

6. How can we understand and use different schemas of things to extend learning towards magnified moments of change?

And finally

7. How can we best give learners with complex needs a sense of dignity and SMSC encounter?

Reflection ⑦

Before reading further, take some time to consider these seven questions.

» Which words resonate most for you? Pick three of the seven questions and make notes on your response.

» Are there any questions you would add from your own observations?

Whether training those new to teaching or those more experienced in the classroom, a question I often ask is '*What is your model of learning?*' I strongly believe all teachers and leaders in education effectively need to have a model of learning. This could be an existing theoretical model and/or one they have developed themselves through observation and experience. Please note, I am not referring to the myth that is 'learning styles' but a generic process schema of how shared information transitions into knowledge, skills, experience, application, attitude and eventually wisdom. I have shared mine previously (Devi, 2020, pp 38–9). The importance of this schema is to help find out what is going on when a learner appears not to be learning.

It is important to note that this 'learning' process may take place; however, the most tangible way pupils 'communicate' their learning and progress in the classroom is through speech and written work. In the profession, we call this assessment. In reality, it is feedback from the learner of what they have absorbed, what they have understood, what they can do and what they have connected to previous learning to extend learning. Does this mean those who cannot communicate do not learn? No. Our challenge is to figure out the how and what.

Activate agency

The feedback loop is a critical element of learning. However, this does not occur in isolation or without complexity. Nutbrown (2011) puts forward the case that babies use their sense during an encounter to discover, solve puzzles, socially connect and communicate. These pre-school experiences help shape their schemas of thinking. Quoting Atley (2007), Nutbrown (2011) recognises these schemas as below-the-surface behaviour root patterns that connect content, context and experience. Subsequently through repetition, they result in categories and logical classifications seen above the surface. In theory, therefore, we all have a schema of thinking.

Imagine the classroom situation shown in Figure 7.1.

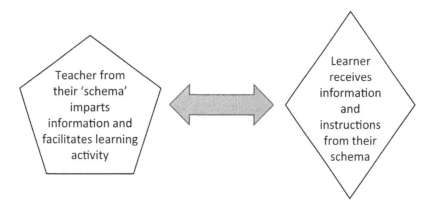

Figure 7.1 *Exchange of information and ideas between teacher and learner*

Application 🔡

» Think about how you can use an understanding of different pupils' schemas to teach more effectively in your classroom. One way I have done this in the past is to use person-centred tools to deepen my understanding of the learner's voice. I particularly advocate the One Page Profile (Devi, 2020).

A question that emerges from this is, therefore, who or what determines continuity and progress? Policy, the adult, the learner, hidden thought or continued exchange of understanding and meaningful dialogue?

CASE STUDY ☻

Does feedback in learning matter?

The human body and brain are designed to work in a continual feedback loop. Interpreting the signals and acting upon them becomes one challenge. However, a bigger and different challenge is when signals are lost or miscommunicated. Recently, a mother took her teenage son to hospital to discover her son had broken the bones in his hands over a year ago. The break was significant and, undetected over the year, had become significantly worse. After several different tests and investigations, it was discovered this boy (and his brothers) have a congenital insensitivity to pain and anhidrosis (CIPA). Basically, they do not feel pain or temperature and have decreased levels of sweat. So, the experience is there and real, but the 'feeling' sensation and communication thereof of such experiences is not. It is equally possible to have scenarios where children experience 'pain' but cannot communicate to anyone that they are in pain.

There are no easy answers, but it does highlight the importance of communication and feedback in the learning cycle. As such we need to be intentional in providing tools for students to communicate needs, wants and feelings. Equally, we cannot assume learning is not taking place when nothing is said or communicated. With non-verbal children, I have found letting them lead and show me helps. However, this kind of interaction requires an investment of both space and time.

It starts with creating space. In a class of 30, in a mainstream setting, I would use objects, photos, colours, structures and something we called 'Bubble Time' to create definitive opportunities for students to communicate. Consider the reflective ideas below – would any work in your classroom?

Reflection ⑦

» **Objects:** A tray of objects, where students could choose what they wanted to touch and handle would give me a window into their schema of thinking. As they picked an object up and explored it, I would respond, '*Show me*'. They would twist and turn the object, sometimes pointing with their eyes at what fascinated them. For children with co-ordination difficulties, I would slowly rotate the object, watching for changes in their eye movement or body language indicating interest. My language was directed through questions and direct commands. Progress was measured through increased 'points of interest' or stronger communicative signals. For those with some speech, it was about extended patterns of speech and connection of said object to other learning or objects. Often the objects were great ways to form connections with others (social).

» **Photographs:** Language development involves a progression from 3D objects to photographs (2D exact replicas) to pictures (2D interpretations) to symbols and icons and finally words, where contextual meaning helps learners discern whether the word 'treasure', for example, refers to a noun or a verb. Language is complex and full of nuances. Photographs help bridge what is 'heard' with what is 'seen'. Photographs can lead to structured writing activities, again dependent on the situation. However, they also can support emotive understanding around the subject, as well as the learner's response to the stimulus – moving from simple distinctions of like/dislike to '*This makes me feel ...*' With social media, we are living in an increasingly visual world and so intentionally connecting words to imagery is powerful.

» **Colours:** Feelings are often hard to describe, but you could use a colour fan and ask a learner, '*What colour are you feeling today?*' This isn't a question with a right or wrong answer, but is just a doorway into deeper conversation. If a child chose blue from the colour fan, I would follow up with, '*What does that mean for you?*' This approach re-enforces the power of choice.

» **Structures:** Recording work doesn't have to be linear. A wide range of visual representations such as tree diagrams, Venn diagrams and flow charts can be used. The structures lend themselves to the learner showing their learning. I have used these, and children have drawn their responses to show learning, or they have sorted objects and pictures within a structure. This is useful for demonstrating different aspects of culture – in other words, aspects that are similar and areas that are distinct and different. These help to identify internal schemas of thinking that have yet to manifest into logical classifications.

» **Bubble Time:** This was an established classroom routine, where once independent work had been set, learners could come and talk to me about things in their hearts and on their minds. There was a signalling system for the pupils to indicate they needed this, and all the others respected that while I was talking to this pupil, they were not to disturb us. We were in our 'Bubble Space'. Everyone had access, and everyone valued the choice they had to use it or not.

Reflection ⑦

» Take a moment to sit at a learner's desk in your classroom. What do you see, hear, smell and touch? Does the environment lend itself to increased learning communications and deeper learning conversations? What could be better?

CASE STUDY

We live in a world where often we are overwhelmed by choice. Look at the chocolate or cereal aisle in a supermarket, for example. For Tom, information overload was real. He needed to simply be given two options and for him to choose one. This is known as fixed choices. In other words, the number of options is limited, but the learner is still making a choice. Mumta was also in Tom's class; her learning thrived on choice. Their class teacher decided to differentiate the work by using choice boards. Tom was given a 1×2 structure and Mumta was given a 3×3. These could be used to help children make moral or spiritual choices.

Table 7.1 *Two different choice boards used in the same lesson (Tom 1×2) and Mumta (3×3)*

A	B

1	2	3
4	5	6
7	8	9

Reflection ⑦

Think back to a lesson you taught last week.

» How was choice incorporated into the lesson?

» Did you consider how many choices to offer?

» What would you do differently in hindsight?

Breakthrough

CASE STUDY 🔊

Ohashi and Ostry (2021) highlight how the speech development aspect of the brain lends itself to neuroplasticity. In a study published in the same year, Fiori et al (2021) demonstrated that treatment for speech apraxia brought about neural changes for children. The point here being that a condition or label isn't static.

As educators, we are not speech therapists or specialists in this area. However, we can, as Nutbrown (2011) highlights, contribute to continuity, consistency and progression.

When asked to observe learning in a classroom, I'm always keen to record the teacher talk time: student talk time ratio. I've mostly taught in areas of social deprivation. Leaving my class at the end of the day, many of my learners would not speak out loud to another person until they returned to school the next morning. So, I had to intentionally make opportunities for talk. I had to consider scaffolding talk time as well as the pairing of individuals. We found the more reluctant communicator or those with speech impediments felt 'safe' to start expressing their ideas – sometimes through just one word but moving more towards full sentences.

Reflection ⑦

» How would you describe the language interaction in your classroom?

» Are you modelling good speech patterns? How?

» How much airtime is given to students to speak and articulate their thoughts and ideas?

CASE STUDY 🔊

Jonathan Bryan (see photo below) has complex needs. He was labelled as having profound and multiple needs (PMLD) at four years old, when he entered the education system. Starved of oxygen in the womb when his mother was in a car accident, Jonathan has severe cerebral palsy, and is quadriplegic, oxygen dependent and non-verbal. He is now a young adult and at the time of writing has applied to attend university. Jonathan is a great advocate that all children, regardless of their needs, should be taught to read and write. Jonathan communicates through his eyes. He has written a book and can confidently communicate his ideas and thoughts to others.

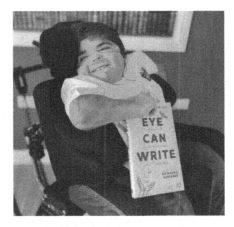

The following upside-down poem in his book *Eye Can Write* (2018) by Jonathan (aged 12 at the time) highlights how powerful his voice can be.

PMLD

We are not capable of learning
So do not tell me
There's something going on behind the disability.
Treated as useless handicaps
Minds with nothing in there, tragically
Stuck in a wheelchair,
Disabilities visibly crippling -
Just incontinent and dribbling,
We are not
Academically able.
You should make our minds
Stagnate in special education!
We cannot
Learn to read,
Learn to spell,
Learn to write,
Instead let us
Be constrained by a sensory curriculum.
It is not acceptable to say
We have the capacity to learn.
School should occupy us, entertain us; but never teach us
You are deluded to believe that
Our education can be looked at another way!

(now read from bottom to top)

© Jonathan Bryan

Figure 7.2 *Jonathan Bryan's poem, PMLD, in his book* Eye Can Write, *2018*

Talking to Jonathan's mother about his journey, I realised that from fixed choices of letters/words, using the etran (eye movement selection method), breakthrough came when Jonathan learnt to spell. In Jonathan's own words:

> I learnt to read using a whole word reading method and started to write choosing whole words. When I learnt to spell, I could spell out everything I wanted to write and say – it unlocked my voice.

As a class teacher, I used to tell my pupils, 'You learn to read, so that one day you can read to learn'. The latter opens up a world of possibilities for pupils because they can learn anything! This was the moment for Jonathan; as he learnt to spell, words and communication opened up to him in a way no one could have predicted or expected. Jonathan attended a special school until he was seven, undertaking literacy and maths studies at home for part of the day. At age nine he enrolled in a local mainstream school and went on to attend secondary mainstream schools.

Reflection ⑦

» What breakthrough moments are needed in your classroom for your learners?

» How can you facilitate a different way of learning?

» Do you have some pupils stuck in a fixed mode that need to be stretched to open up independent learning to them?

Clarity on personal identity

SMSC education does impact identity. We do not live in a vacuum and children and young people without speech require social, moral, spiritual and cultural encounters. Consistency and continuity appear to be the key. Recently in a church setting, Farukh (name anonymised), who is wheelchair bound with limited speech and movement, lifted his arm to indicate that he wanted someone to come and pray with him. Someone stepped forward and held Farukh's hands. He held on tight and though he couldn't say/sing all the words, he sang along to the worship song. He knew reverence of the lyrics and so he looked down the whole time, not letting go of the person. At the end of the song, he naturally let go, content that his spiritual soul had had an encounter.

There is so much we do not know about this world and human potential. In this moment, Farukh experienced something. We cannot label it and he cannot articulate it. But something changed for him. Re-read Jonathan's poem – how much of his identity can you see in his words?

Some books published to support delivery of SMSC education advocate the simplification of language for those with communication needs or even reducing the curriculum. In doing so, are we doing our learners a disservice?

Reflection ⑦

> » Do we restrict the potential of individuals with labels just because they do not fit our expectations?

> » Equally, do we restrict the growth of those who cannot articulate their own path of continuity and growth?

Connectivity

Look again at the cyclical wheel from Chapter 1. Does breakthrough bring the agency or agency lead to breakthrough? This is not a causal or sequential model. It is, however, a consequential one. Agency, breakthrough and clarity all impact each other.

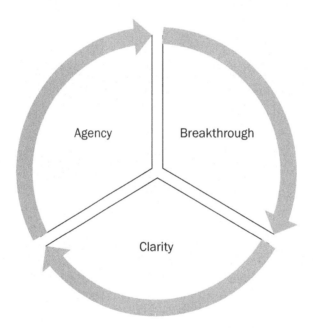

Figure 7.3 *ABC consequential connectivity*

Most countries have a national curriculum and key milestones they want learners to achieve. But within those are micro-moments of change that if magnified can produce breakthrough moments of learning.

Magnified moments of change occur when you intentionally understand your learners' schema of thought, as well as your own and the interaction between the two. They also occur when you pursue deeper knowledge about identity. Stating someone is 'unique' isn't enough. How have they been made or wired? What are you doing as a practitioner to bring out 'excellence' in them?

Classrooms shape everyone in them on a daily basis. Think about how a challenging pupil has improved or changed the way you teach. Being open to new methods and possibilities is what makes working in education one of the most exciting opportunities.

I came into education to give all learners a sense of pride and dignity in who they are and what they could become. The curriculum is a vehicle to make that happen. It is a means to an end, not the end in itself. As a teacher, I soon realised SMSC education was pivotal to all the other subjects and character development. Communicating through his spelling board, Jonathan demonstrated a great sense of humour.

Sensory sensitivity is only half the story. True learning happens through self-awareness and that is as much about individuals knowing who they are as knowing who others are.

Summary

This chapter has explored seven questions around the three constructs of agency, breakthrough and clarity (ABC) in relation to limited communication and the SMSC curriculum. I have provided case studies, research, personal examples and challenging questions to extend reflective thought in the classroom. I have provided a schema exchange model of learning (Figure 7.1), differentiating choice boards (Table 7.1) and a reminder of consequential connectivity (Figure 7.3). Finally, I have set a basis for relating this to other chapters, in particular Chapters 4 and 6.

Reflection ⑦

» What are your key takeaways from this chapter and how will you apply them to yourself and others?

Key takeaways 📖

It is my hope that you take away the following seven ideas from this chapter.

1. While speech can accelerate learning, those without speech or the ability to write can still learn.

2. Choice matters and different opportunities can be created in the classroom to facilitate this.

3. Creating new neural pathways in the brain is possible.

4. Learning breakthroughs require you as a practitioner to think outside the box.

5. Delivery of SMSC education needs to go beyond language to address the core of defining personal identity.

6.   Within the national curriculum milestones, seek out magnified moments of change that can act as a catalyst for greater continuity and progression.

7.   Make time to consider learner pride and dignity and how to encourage this in your classroom.

Further reading

- Eye Can Talk (nd) About Me. [online] Available at: https://eyecantalk.net/about (accessed 22 July 2024).
- Teach Us Too (nd) [online] Available at: www.teachustoo.org.uk (accessed 22 July 2024).

References

Bryan, J (2018) *Eye Can Write: A Memoire of a Child's Silent Soul Emerging*. London: Bonnier Publishing.

Devi, A (2020) *Essential Guides for Early Career Teachers: Special Educational Needs and Disability*. St Albans: Critical Publishing.

Fiori, S, Pannek, K, Podda, I, Cipriani, P, Lorenzoni, V, Franchi, B, Pasquariello, R, Guzzetta, A, Cioni, G and Chilosi, A (2021) Neural Changes Induced by a Speech Motor Treatment in Childhood Apraxia of Speech: A Case Series. *Journal of Child Neurology*, 36(11): 958–67.

Nutbrown, C (2011) *The Threads of Thinking*. London: Sage Publications.

Ohashi, H and Ostry, D J (2021) Neural Development of Speech Sensorimotor Learning. *The Journal of Neuroscience*, 41(18): 4023–35.

Speech and Language UK (2023) *Listening to Unheard Children*. [online] Available at: https://speechandlanguage.org.uk/the-issue/our-campaigns/listening-to-unheard-children (accessed 22 July 2024).

Epilogue

ANITA DEVI

May none be lost.

John, 17

This is one of my favourite prayers in The Bible, which in many ways sums up the heart of this book. No child or young person should be lost in our education system. We know needs are changing and increasing, year on year. We also know resources are not increasing at the same rate. They can't. However, effective provision to meet diverse needs isn't just about doing more. It is about doing things differently. Difference is not a dirty word. In our pursuit of inclusion, we have lost the beauty of difference. Difference lends itself to personalisation. Each of us, I believe, is 'fearfully and wonderfully' made, as the Psalmists would say. Here, fearfully implies 'with awe and for awe'. As a classroom practitioner, I have never ceased to marvel with awe at my students: the questions they ask, they ideas they share, the creative solutions they suggest, the art they create, the laughter they bring, the words they write and the kindness they show. We live in world where attainment has become standardised. The initial intent behind this policy was to ensure all children received a high-quality standard of education, regardless of where they were educated or who they were educated by. A noble idea, but overemphasis on the measurement of the 'standard' through assessment came at a price. What we lost was valuing the awe of how each individual child has been created with purpose, a personality and character. There was a secondary loss in the system from standardisation: we lost the children. Education was no longer about discovery but about facts and long-term economic outcomes. If children didn't meet the standard, a process of labelling 'the problem' followed. From labels came generalisation and stereotyping. It all started to spiral. In this process, we lost the teachers too.

But change is coming!

It's time to claim back our classrooms as intentional spaces of 'awe and wonder' and personal discovery. Imagine a world, where at the end of each day, we knew we had learnt something from our interactions, we had discovered something about ourselves, and we had contributed to the personal development of each other. Imagine the contentment. As the sun set and the stars adorned the night sky, we could say, '*It is good; it is very good*'. This affirmation would not, I believe, bring about complacency, but encouragement from what has been (the past and today) and anticipation for what more could be (tomorrow). The end of the day would be a cliffhanger for learning more. We would be building stronger foundations for future generations. When training teachers, I have always shared that education has the unique presence to connect the time continuum of past, present and future through different people, an enriched purposeful curriculum and an interactive growth dialogue. In the present, we let go of guilt and shame of the past and we stand confidently, not worrying about the future. In that moment we know, this is where we are meant to be. There is both contentment and expectation of greater things to come.

This book is not the end, but the beginning

It's the beginning of how you apply what you have read and learnt. It is the beginning of asking deeper questions. We have only scratched the surface in this book. Our hope has been to move away from focusing solely on needs and diagnosis, but to use this and our relationship with our learners to build up 'personalised profiles' of who they are and who they are created to be. We chose to focus not on dead ends, but on building pathways and highways that are designed to last, through lived-out wisdom. Every child and young person has been created with a purpose and an amazing destiny of fulfilment. Our role as educators is to enable them along their path as best we can. Of course you will make mistakes, of course you don't have all the answers and of course it is not your sole responsibility. But teaching has never been about 'knowing it all'; it has always been about 'enabling all'. This is the ancient pathway built for endurance.

Teaching is a privilege

It is a vocation, and in choosing this path you take an oath to ensure all those placed in our classrooms make progress. Your job is to facilitate a process of personal and continuous growth that sustains lifelong learning. This is the ecology of learning. You cannot do it alone, which is why the schools that adopt a team approach to support neurodivergent needs are the ones that thrive and flourish. If you want your learners to actively make wise choices and decisions, you need to model agency in your everyday interactions. You need to give them a voice and you need to make time to truly listen. This may involve digging deeper to join the dots or going further to support success through breakthrough moments. But it is worth it, because then each child will walk confidently in their own identity. Every chapter in this book gives you tools, strategies and examples of what could be. But there is more for you to discover beyond this book.

My encouragement to you all

Observe, notice, reflect, try, discover and record what you see happening in your classroom. Place the learner back at the centre of the learning process, not just in words, but actively see the world through their eyes, hear the world through their ears and understand the world through their hearts. That's when you enter into the classroom ambience of 'awe and wonder'. In the long term, these learners will carry awe and wonder into adulthood, and you will see far more than just economic outcomes. You will see the fruition of life for all in different aspects of society and community engagement.

Thank you for making the time to read this book and to revisit it over and over in order to shape and develop your classroom environment for personal discovery, so that one day instead of the prayer, '*May none be lost*', we will declare '***In our classrooms, all are found***'.

This is our dream. This is our hope.

> *May all children be lost in the awe and mystery of educational discovery and found in the power of love and learning!*

Appendix for Chapter 5

Developmental norms 4–11 years

(*Always consider the opportunities a child has had to be presented with opportunities to practise skills as well)

Age	Language & reading development	Physical & motor development	Social & emotional development	Cognitive development	Red flags
4 yrs	• Uses correct grammar most of the time. • Can recognise rhymes. • Can sit and listen to a story for five minutes. • Infantile substitutions in speech. • Understands number/space concepts – eg on/over/under.	**Gross motor** • Dressing self unaided (except tying shoelaces). • Uses whole body to kick ball forcibly. • Catches large ball between extended arms. • Jumps vertically with both feet leaving the floor. • Goes downstairs one foot per step. **Fine motor** • Can copy and draw a cross, horizontal and vertical line. • Can button and unbutton own clothing. • Can thread beads. • Can cut paper with scissors.	• Can play with other children and take turns. • Observing others in play.	• Asks lots of questions. • Gives first and last name. • Can repeat three digits correctly – three times, eg six–eight–nine. • Counts to 20. • Can watch a TV programme or DVD for 10 minutes.	• **No pointing at items or people.** • **Little or no understandable 3+ word sentences.** • **Hard for others to understand speech.** • **Difficulty running/climbing.** • **Dribbling.** • **Difficulty with nursery rhymes.**

(Cont.)

Developmental norms 4–11 years

(*Always consider the opportunities a child has had to be presented with opportunities to practise skills as well)

5 yrs					
	• Engages appropriately in conversations. • Uses 'would' or 'could' appropriately. • Able to identify and name all uppercase and lowercase letters. • Uses sentences containing at least seven or eight words. • Uses past tense more consistently. • Describes objects. • Speech fluent with few infantile substitutions.	**Gross motor** • Riding a bicycle with training wheels. • Can walk along a narrow line heel to toe. • Climbs play equipment. • Able to jump to a height of about 30 cm. • Can go up and down stairs alternating feet. • Shows improvements in running and jumping. • Can catch a large ball with their hands. • Can attend to toilet needs without much help. **Fine motor** • Cutting across a page with scissors. • Copies their own name. • Colours within the lines. • Can hold a pen or pencil in tripod or equivalent grip.	• Choosing friends and co-operating in play. • Prefers playing in small groups. • Protects younger children. • Shows respect for other people's property. • Plays well without the need for constant adult supervision. • Understands the nature of giving and receiving. • Can turn take. • Separates from mother easily. • Gives appropriate eye contact – eg when being spoken to. • Sitting at the table for ten minutes.	• Uses imagination to create stories. • Can match colours. • Can listen to a story for ten minutes. • Can name the seven days in a week. • Has a vocabulary of over 2000 words. • Can recognise numerals, at least 1–5. • When asked can say their own name and address.	• **Deterioration in motor function, eg walking, running.** • **Not turn-taking, playing with other children.** • **Not counting to ten.** • **Not able to do rhyming songs.** • **Limited vocabulary.** • **Can't sit still compared with other children of similar age.** • **Aggressive behaviour towards others.**

Developmental norms 4–11 years

(*Always consider the opportunities a child has had to be presented with opportunities to practise skills as well)

6 yrs		**Gross motor**			
• Talks fluently. • Can understand more complex grammatical rules. • Can read and write to some degree. • Can learn how to do things through the use of language. • Can use language to work through scenarios and problems.	• Can cut and stick. • Can copy basic 2D shapes (eg square, triangle, diamond). • Can use a knife to spread jam/butter, etc. • Brushes teeth (but may need reminding).	• Able to control speed when running and avoid collision. • Can jump down several steps. • Can kick a football up to 6 m away. • Can throw a ball with accuracy. • Able to stand and balance on one foot for at least three seconds. • Walks heel-to-toe in a straight line. • Dresses and undresses without help. • Brushes own hair well.	• Expresses awareness of others' feelings. • Enjoys imaginative play with other children. • Can be selfish or overly competitive. • May still have tantrum behaviours. • Gets upset when criticised by others.	• Is inquisitive. • Can take others' perspectives. • More emphasis on quantity rather than quality of work. • Enjoys starting tasks but these are not always completed. • Can distinguish reality from something that is made up. • Can give reasons. • Can follow directions. • Can do addition and subtraction of single digits.	• **Can't copy shapes.** • **Spelling errors for one-syllable words.** • **Difficulty turn-taking.** • **Speech not fluent.**

(Cont.)

Developmental norms 4–11 years

(*Always consider the opportunities a child has had to be presented with opportunities to practise skills as well)

7 yrs	• Can describe points of similarity between two objects. • Should understand opposite analogies easily (eg black–white, big–small, beginning–end).	• Rides a bike without stabilisers. • Catches and bounces a small ball four to six times. **Fine motor** • Tying shoelaces. • Using a knife and fork correctly. • Drawing a diamond. • Can draw a person. • Cuts out shapes well using scissors. • Can open and close a zip. • Writes their first and last name. **Gross motor** • Can ride a bicycle without training wheels. • Can walk along a thin line. • Can do a somersault or forward roll.	• Can wait their turn during an activity. • Desires to be perfect and is self-critical. • Starts to look for independence.	• Can understand the rules of a game. • Has a reasonable attention span (20 minutes).	• **Not reading aloud to others with fluency.** • **Not able to do syllable breakdown.** • **Obsessional behaviour.**

(Cont.)

(*Cont.*)

Developmental norms 4–11 years

(*Always consider the opportunities a child has had to be presented with opportunities to practise skills as well)

• Should be able to read aloud to some extent. • Able to use an increasing number of words and understand more concepts.	• Can catch skilfully using one hand. • Is able to throw skilfully using one hand. • Able to plan movements. • Has an awareness of direction and distance. • Shows improvements in hand–eye co-ordination. **Fine motor** • Is able to cut using a knife. • Can draw a diagonal line.	• Moods can fluctuate. • Has more of an awareness of their own emotions. • Worries about not being liked by others. • Tends to complain more often. • Shows strong emotional reactions. • Worries more – may have low self-confidence. • Is a better loser and is less likely to place blame.	• Uses serious logical thinking – can be thoughtful and reflective. • Can tell the time (including quarter of an hour) with ease. • Knows the days, months and seasons. • Able to solve more complex problems. • Is able to understand the difference between right and wrong. • Can understand at least three separate instructions within a command. • Can remember which hand is left and which is right.	**• Limited interaction with other children.** **• Difficulty with motor tasks – gross or fine motor – not catching/ throwing accurately/not copying shapes accurately.**

→

Developmental norms 4–11 years

(*Always consider the opportunities a child has had to be presented with opportunities to practise skills as well)

8 yrs	• Can converse at an almost adult level. • Can read with confidence and fluency. • Reading may be a major interest. • Can use complex sentences with ease. • Has established all sounds used in speech. • Has control over aspects of reading aloud such as rate, pitch and volume. • Can follow more complex commands.	**Gross motor** • Can bathe themselves. • Can pour a drink without spilling. • Needs to be physically active every day (approx. 30 minutes). **Fine motor** • Uses a ruler.	• Emotions change quickly. • Impatient – finds waiting for special events tortuous. • Makes friends easily; develops close friends, usually of same sex. • Favours group play, clubs and team sports – wants to feel part of a group. • More influenced by peer pressure. • Has a strong need for love and understanding – especially from primary carer.	• Knows of and can explain the uses of a number of objects. • Has a short-term memory repetition of at least three numbers. • Can sit and concentrate for 15–20 minutes. • Seeks to understand the reasons for things. • Begins to feel competent in skills and have preferences for some activities and subjects. • Thinking is organised and logical. • Begins to recognise concept of reversibility (4 + 2 = 6 and 6 – 2 = 4). • Can do some simple division and multiplication.	• **Difficulties using scissors/rulers.**

(Cont.)

Developmental norms 4–11 years

(*Always consider the opportunities a child has had to be presented with opportunities to practise skills as well)

9 yrs		
• Likes to talk and share ideas.	**Gross motor** • Can help make a snack or drink for him or herself.	• Can be helpful, cheerful and pleasant as well as rude, bossy and selfish. • May be quite sensitive and overly dramatic. • Can be obsessed with and motivated by money. • Can keep secrets. • Can articulate their feelings. • Usually enjoys school – doesn't enjoy being absent from school. • Is possessive of their belongings. • Has a best friend. • May experience wide mood swings.
	• Writes stories.	• **Writing difficulties.**

Developmental norms 4–11 years

(*Always consider the opportunities a child has had to be presented with opportunities to practise skills as well)

		Fine motor • Can use a computer keyboard/mobile phone.	• May be critical of self and others. • Often dislikes the opposite sex intensely. • Puts great importance on fairness – for self and others. • Responsible – can be depended upon and trusted.	• May use physical complaints to avoid unpleasant tasks.	
10 yrs	• Reads to learn (rather than learning to read).	**Gross motor** • Interested in own strength. • Has both skill and stamina for gross motor activities such as biking, skating and team sports. **Fine motor** • Capable of fine hand and finger movements. • Draws with great detail.	• Still certain that own beliefs are correct and are universally shared. • Disposition is generally happy, sometimes silly. • Respectful and affectionate towards both parents.	• Can buy something in a shop and handle money. • Has a strong desire to complete tasks – may persist with an activity until exhausted. • Memorises and recites facts – but may not show deep understanding.	• **Writing not fluent and easy for others to read.** • **Frequent spelling errors.** • **Difficulty remaining in seat in class.** • **Aggression to others in unstructured settings.**

(Cont.)

Developmental norms 4–11 years

(*Always consider the opportunities a child has had to be presented with opportunities to practise skills as well)

	• Good keyboard skills on computer.	• Uses tools, such as a hammer, can opener or small garden tools, fairly well.	• Fears which were previously bothersome are now minimal. • May anger quickly but expression of anger differs according to the situation. • Friendships are quite important – friends are often of the same sex. • Enjoys socialising in clubs and group activities.	• Keeps train of thought and will continue work even after interruptions. • Able to use a dictionary or order things alphabetically. • Critical thinking starting to emerge. • Developing a conscience but not yet consistently able to tell right from wrong. • Aware of time but needs help to plan time in a practical way. • Can do percentages.	• **Few friends.**
11 yrs		• Can make a snack.	• Self-care – wash/ brush teeth. • Can help lay and clear the table.	• Can write a story competently. • Beginning to be aware of right and wrong (versus good and bad).	• **Writing not fluent and easy for others to read.** • **Reluctant to write.** • **Frequent spelling errors.**

(Cont.)

Developmental norms 4–11 years

(*Always consider the opportunities a child has had to be presented with opportunities to practise skills as well)

• Starts to realise that others may hold beliefs different from own. • Displays anger physically – fights, slams doors, kicks. • Away from home, behaviour is well mannered and quite helpful. • Friendships are still important but with more quarrels than before. • May have one or two 'best friends'.	• Can sit at the table for 30 minutes. • Can work independently doing homework. • Able to use logic in arguments and apply logic to specific, concrete situations. • Combines oral, visual and written material in school reports. • Shows improvements in ability to make decisions. • Can do simple word maths problems. • Can understand concept of fractions – whole/half/quarter. • Can start to combine two shapes to make a new shape.	• **Difficulty remaining in seat in class.** • ***Aggression to others in unstructured settings.*** • **Few friends – not invited to social events by others.**

Index

Note: Page numbers in italics denote figures and tables.